the *inner* world of JIMI HENDRIX

by his fiancée MONIKA DANNEMANN

BLAZING GENIUS

the inner world of JIMI HENDRIX

by his fiancée MONIKA DANNEMANN

St. Martin's Press
New York

First published in Great Britain 1995
Bloomsbury Publishing Plc, 2 Soho Square,
London W1V 6HB

The author and publishers have made every effort
to contact all copyright holders. Any who for any
reason have not been contacted are invited to
write to the publishers so that a full
acknowledgement may be made in subsequent
editions of this work

ISBN 0-312-137-389
First U.S. Edition: September 1995
10 9 8 7 6 5 4 3 2 1

Designed by Bradbury and Williams
Printed by Butler & Tanner Ltd., Frome and London

CONTENTS

INTRODUCTION

Jimi Hendrix had a vast mind. He was without doubt one of the most original, most inspired artists who ever lived.

This book is a visual and verbal record of Jimi as seen through the eyes of the woman he trusted most, Monika. It is not a kiss-and-tell story; nor is it a biography. Instead, it is a collection of truly inspired paintings and writings by Monika which were designed to express and complement Jimi's message in a unique visual form.

Jimi's music has a timeless quality which defies description. His music and words are as relevant today as they were back then — only in a different way. He is constantly being "rediscovered" by successive generations and this will continue for a very long time to come. This is why Monika's book is so important, because it adds a vital and positive dimension to the Hendrix legacy and because her paintings share the timelessness and universality of his music. The way she depicts Jimi reflects her deep understanding as well as her true love for him.

Monika's book is not concerned with the physical aspects of the man, but strives to fathom the invisible, the mysterious facets of Jimi's personality and to reveal the person behind the image. In concentrating on Jimi's message, it shines new light on the true meaning of his words. This is the first book to touch convincingly on the inner world of Jimi Hendrix — a world of natural magic, of fairy tales, and of some of the deepest mysteries of human experience. It delves into worlds beyond the visible, tangible plane — into the metaphysical — and tells of Jimi's breathtaking visions of heaven and hell, of future, past and present, and of long-forgotten continents and civilizations.

One thing that is evident throughout this book is that Jimi had a tremendous pool of inner wisdom and used his senses and his considerable metaphysical intelligence in a special way. He felt that he was guided towards a higher purpose, that he was here ultimately to help others too to find themselves in their own way.

Despite all his otherworldliness, which he tended to keep hidden from the gaze of the public, Jimi was gifted with an astute realism which penetrated the complex web of social interactions. In some of his later interviews, it is amazing how clearly he saw through the phoney mechanisms of society and how he was not afraid to expose them. Whereas many just complained about their lot in life, Jimi sought positive alternatives, and new ways of looking at things.

It also becomes clear in this book that Jimi felt people did not understand him. It is generally accepted that few got really close to him, although he was at the centre of a maelstrom of people swirling around him almost constantly. There were very few people, less than a handful, that he ever really opened up to. And among these Monika was the one Jimi chose to explain the meaning of his lyrics to and to share his thinking and convictions with. Jimi felt a strong desire to share this knowledge, but until meeting Monika he had not sensed the right kind of feedback from other people to encourage him to open up about these things.

Jimi's love for Monika had an extra dimension: he saw in her his soul mate and he was completely delighted by her genuine desire to and readiness to share his mysterious world with him. In return, she repaid him with total enthusiasm and commitment, which he sensed from her and which gave him strength, as well as hope, for the future.

It is true that Monika entered Jimi's life rather late, some eighteen months before his death, and, because of a whole array of circumstances, they were forced to be apart for most of that time. But it is also true that this was the period of the mature Jimi, who had left behind the "wild man" stage image that had been fabricated for him and was in search of a new approach. So, while Monika may not have experienced all sides of Jimi's multifaceted character, she certainly saw and valued many of his most hidden qualities.

There are many people who spend their lives with others, but still don't know much about what their partner is really like inside. On the other hand, some people are on the same wavelength, open up to each other instantly and experience a very deep understanding and natural rapport which others don't achieve in a lifetime.

This special rapport is particularly evident in Monika's painting, which are true masterpieces in the traditional sense of the world. They eerily capture the essence of Jimi and what he stands for, and in her portraits we can sense his soul looking directly at us.

Twenty-five years ago Monika promised Jimi, on his insistence, that she would help to spread his message. With this book she is fulfilling that promise.

U.J. Roth
England, March 1995

ELECTRIC CHURCH

FOREWORD

For a long time now a plan has been maturing in me to publish a book about Jimi Hendrix: a book which would reveal that aspect of him which is so rarely mentioned — the inner world of Jimi Hendrix.

However, being a rather private person, I had great difficulty in opening myself to the world and disclosing the private conversations and dreams I shared with Jimi. I did attempt written manuscripts a few times, but because of complicated circumstances, never finished them. Meanwhile what struck me forcibly over the years was that the spiritual side of Jimi was strangely absent from all the books on him that I came across.

The idea of writing a book about Jimi's message first came to me soon after his death in 1970. It was very hurtful to see all the falsehoods and misunderstandings about Jimi that were being circulated at that time and I wanted to set the record straight. Because I had been unable to complete a manuscript, I put aside the idea of publishing a book. Anyway, the time did not feel right. Something told me it would be better to wait.

Then, unexpectedly, after not having thought about a book for many years, a new way forward began to appear, and this time it felt right. So eventually the book was completed in a very short period of time. It does not contain all the things that Jimi taught me. But it has all the most important ones and a lot of it is based directly on my first original manuscript, written back in 1970.

Through the following oil paintings and commentaries, I intend to show and explain the essence of many conversations I had with Jimi. Each commentary serves as a guide to Jimi's personality, as well as to the accompanying painting.

Although I have deliberately emphasized Jimi's spiritual side, it would be quite wrong to imagine that I want to put him on a pedestal, to make him an object of worship. For Jimi was not a saint, but a real person, albeit a very charismatic and evolved one. Like anyone else, he had his flaws, and made mistakes in his life, but he was nevertheless a man of truly great talent and exceptional qualities.

In the last two years of his short life, Jimi's spirituality came increasingly into the open — a fact which seems to have been comprehensively overlooked. And yet any journalist who gave him the space to speak freely will confirm that it was at such moments that the real Jimi came through, outlining breathtaking projects for the future and talking passionately about issues close to his heart.

Jimi was not granted enough time to alter the skilfully manipulated image which had been thrust upon him by his management, the media and in some respects also by himself. Having understood the great damage that this false impression had done to his personal reputation and his artistic credibility, during the last two years of his life he struggled to rectify it. But all his efforts were undermined by his management and others, keenly aware that it was this very image which brought in the money.

In the years after his death in 1970, no forceful voice was heard in Jimi's defence. I tried to speak up for him many times, but only a few people seemed to want to listen. His reputation was dragged further and further into the gutter by books and the press, which bolstered still further the sensationalism and opportunism of those striving for their own ends.

I believe it is my destiny to help reveal Jimi's personal and spiritual essence — the side of him which he felt to be the most important, and the side which he used to say I knew better than anyone else. More than once he expressed to me his regret that only a handful of the people he had met were really interested in this philosophy and spiritual knowledge. I should point out that anyone who knows, or thinks, that he or she has a real and deep understanding of Jimi should not feel excluded by what I say in this book. On the contrary, I would love to share Jimi's spiritual legacy with as many genuinely interested people as possible.

Jimi was an exceptional person. It was therefore difficult to understand him without thoroughly tuning into his ways of thinking and feeling. In order to really appreciate Jimi's music in all its deeper aspects, I believe one has to understand the man and the spirit behind the guitar and the image. This is what I aim to convey in this book: my oil paintings of Jimi, in trying to capture his spiritual essence, also endeavour to interpret his personality and his music.

As an artist, I have always found it particularly rewarding to paint Jimi, and not only because of my special relationship with him. His colourful and ever-changing appearance would probably make him an attractive subject for any artist. What I always found especially fascinating was that his face – and this is something I noticed when we were together – seemed to change often, especially when he was playing his guitar. As he went through

different states of mind and emotion, his expression would reflect the various influences which were inspiring him. This multiplicity of expressions made each painting a new challenge, and in trying to bring out the many facets of Jimi, I hope to have created something like a kaleidoscope of his inner world.

A lot of love and tears have gone into this book. The love is my faith that Jimi and his message will succeed; the tears will hopefully water the seeds contained here, so that at last Jimi Hendrix may be done justice, and the truth may blossom.

I would like to express my special gratitude for the help of Zeno Roth, who made a major contribution to the realization of this project. With great dedication he revised and improved my text throughout the development of this book. For his constant support, advice and encouragement, I am very grateful.

The book could never have been written without the love, support and encouragement of my mother.

From the bottom of my heart a big thank you to James "Al" Hendrix, Janie Hendrix Wright and Ayako June Hendrix for their love and support throughout the years.

I can't adequately describe the enormous help and great ideas I received from Uli Jon Roth, who gave me invaluable advice.

A special mention for the tireless support and research assistance of Dan Foster.

A big thank you to Bill Nitopi, especially for assistance in finding new photographs.

My special thanks to my friend Jill White for her encouragement and assistance with the text.

I also extend my thanks to Robert Sillitoe for

typing the manuscript.

In addition I owe a debt of gratitude to all of the following:

Chris, K.-P. Dannemann, Peter Davis, Dede Miller, David Montague, Isabel Sutherland Campbell, Ben Valkhoff, Ralf Winter, my editor Richard Dawes for his attention to detail and his constant understanding and reassurance, my designer Roy Williams for his creative input, and John Price, for his dedicated approach to the task of photographing my paintings for this book.

I also want to thank everyone else who helped and supported me in my project, and my friends Jeff Stein and David Anastasia for their continued support throughout the years since I first met them.

Janie, Ayako June, me and Al.

Jimi's Family

"To whom it may concern

"I would like to state that my son Jimi Hendrix was engaged to Monika Dannemann and that they planned to get married.

"All these slanderous stories written about Monika regarding my son are false.

"They really loved each other and that I know myself and I just want to get the record straight for all times."

James "Al" Hendrix

"Monika, from the moment I saw your paintings, I realized that you had met Jimi not only in body, but in spirit as well. I can only say, from the bottom of my heart, you have remained true to what Jimi was all about — kind, gentle and artistically creative."

James "Al" Hendrix

"Monika, I appreciate all you have done in your quest to keep Jimi's dreams alive. As we all know, Jimi is a true legend, light years ahead of his time. Everyone he touched has a unique memory of him. He expressed his love for God, life and humankind through his music. Now through your artwork we have a window to your spiritual experience with Jimi. God bless you."

JANIE HENDRIX WRIGHT

Jimi's sister

"I am Ayako June Hendrix. Jimi called me his 'New Mom'. Jimi was a nice young man, he was kind, shy, and fun to be around. I loved him like my own son. I miss him and I wish he were still alive. Monika's paintings are beautiful and very much alive. She's like one of the family, I love her like my own daughter."

AYAKO JUNE HENDRIX

Jimi's stepmother

REMEMBERING JIMI

"There's one thing about Jimi nobody ever wants to discuss, the metaphysical Jimi Hendrix. No one's ever touched the surface of the real Jimi Hendrix…"
BILLY COX
Guitar World, September 1985

"Jimi's spirituality, his whole psyche, was that of someone from another planet. He felt that way about himself. He spoke to me many times about these dreams he had and where he went in his sleep last night or the night before — things people don't like to talk about because a lot of people are not ready for it. Most of the time, he spoke about the Supreme Being. He was spiritual, and it came across in his personality.

"There are those who come before the public eye and are commercialized into the consciousness of the masses. We are told they are popular, and we echo, they are popular. Then there are a few who are so intuitively tuned into the universe that they are still influential, even though they are beyond sight. This is immortality, and Jimi Hendrix is immortal. It is exciting to know that the world has yet to truly be exposed to Jimi's genius. Maybe one day the overshadowing rumours that are used by some to cloud his image will be replaced by an understanding of the man I knew — a child of the universe, a guitar master, a warm and gentle soul."
BILLY COX
Guitar Player, May 1989

"What people have perceived of Jimi has been the externals of his life. The unprecedented genius of his music, the candid details of the drugs, the stories of his comings and goings. Appearances are rarely a reflection of the truth. His spirit lives through his music, but I have always been saddened by the lurid hype and the projection of an image that was very far from the nature of this man. Jimi understood that the only thing of lasting value was love. Love is what he poured into the world. Love is how I knew him. He had a deeper prophetic wisdom, he mirrored God's love through his heart, it came to the world in his music and his writings. In fact much of Jimi's work is reflective, rooted in prayer and his searching for higher spiritual ground… In 'Valleys of Neptune' he writes: 'I feel the ocean swaying me, washing away all my pain. See where I used to be wounded, remember the scar? Now you can't see a thing.' (Original draft of 'Purple Haze — Jesus Saves') 'Sticks and stones can't break my soul. But words they sometimes harm me — maybe it's because I'm forever hungry for the truth of Love.' (Personal reflections, 1969) 'Love is trying, Thank the Lord, Thank the Lord.'

"I shared an important part of my life with him. I remember his graciousness, his modesty, his innate goodness. Musically he was never satisfied, always searching for perfection, a higher beauty. He wrote: '…heaven is deep within you…' 'The earth gives and takes away. But my soul will outlive any black day. I wanna be alive when I die.'

"In the end, what is remembered is the love you gave, and in Jimi's case, he remains unforgettable. THE SPIRIT LIVES!"
JUMA SULTAN
Multi-instrumentalist who worked with Jimi

AT JIMI'S GRAVE.

The first time I heard of a band called the Jimi Hendrix Experience was early in 1968, when I was an ice-skating teacher in Geneva, Switzerland. Driving home from the ice-rink one evening, I was listening to Radio Caroline, a pirate radio station. A song they were playing was so strange, and completely different from anything I had heard before. It was "Purple Haze". I loved the music instantly, as it seemed to touch something inside me like no other music had done before. I found out that the writer of the song and the guitarist of the group was Jimi Hendrix, with Mitch Mitchell on drums and Noel Redding playing bass guitar.

The following winter a back injury had temporarily stopped my skating and I was staying at my parents' house in Düsseldorf, Germany. One day I heard that Jimi Hendrix's group was to play in town, and asked my younger brother, Klaus-Peter, who also liked their music, if he would come to see them with me.

The large concert hall was packed. The band actually had to give two concerts that day. When Jimi started to play I was very impressed, realizing that he was an extremely charismatic person and that his guitar-playing was out of this world. Most of the time I just closed my eyes and listened. I wished the concert would never end, as I could have enjoyed his music for hours.

Afterwards Klaus-Peter and I went to our favourite club, Le Pirate. An associate, Baron Reiner von-der-Osten-Sacken, told me that he had invited Jimi, Mitch and Noel to visit the club. Before long they arrived, and my brother and I were invited to join them. I refused, because I was not interested in meeting any of them, especially not Jimi Hendrix. It was true he was a brilliant and gifted guitarist, but he had been portrayed by the press as a raw, uncivilized person – a "wild man". Only a few days before, I had read headlines in one magazine which said, "Jimi Hendrix is coming to town – all you mothers better lock up your daughters."

I loved the music instantly, as it seemed to touch something inside me like no other music.

CRY OF LOVE

15

I certainly didn't want to know a man like this. At that time I was naive enough to believe that newspapers always wrote the truth!

So, rather than join them, I went to another part of the club. They left about an hour later, and the Baron came over to me, saying that he had arranged to meet Jimi, Mitch and Noel at their hotel the next morning to take some pictures. He asked if I could come and bring my mother's camera, as none of his friends owned one with a flash. I refused at first, as it was against my principles to meet people or make a fuss of them just because they were famous. However, the Baron and some of our friends wouldn't take no for an answer, so eventually though reluctantly I agreed to come with the camera.

On 13 January 1969, at 11 a.m., I arrived at the Park Hotel, where my friends were already waiting. We went into the hotel and sat down in the bar. A few minutes later Mitch and Noel joined us. I kept quiet, feeling pretty embarrassed and angry for having allowed myself to get into such a situation. But worse was to come.

Jimi Hendrix walked into the bar, and I was alarmed when I saw him heading straight in my direction, to sit down right next to me. I felt most uncomfortable and nervous – he was the last person I thought I wanted to meet. I didn't look at him, hoping that he would ignore me. Instead he began talking to me, asking if I could speak English, and what my name was. I had to answer, but I wished I could vanish into thin air. While he was talking I noticed that he was wearing a necklace with a piece of green jade, which was almost identical to the one I had on, so I quickly hid mine under my blouse. (Jimi wore this necklace during the last few days of his life.) Then I saw that he was wearing a North American Indian bracelet and ring, similar to ones I

He asked these things in a very gentle, caring and intelligent way: not at all what you would expect from a "wild man".

had put on that day. I thought it was a strange coincidence, but it didn't make me feel any better.

Jimi asked me all sorts of questions, and seemed to want to know everything about me. He asked these things in a very gentle, caring and intelligent way: not at all what you would expect from a "wild man". He asked whether I had a boyfriend. When I told him I hadn't he refused to believe me at first, until I explained to him that I was only interested in someone that I could really love. After a while he asked, "Do you want to be my girlfriend?"

I was stunned and thought I couldn't be hearing right, but he repeated the question, and added, "I want you to be my girlfriend and my lady. I've been searching for you for a long time." I couldn't believe that he was serious and said, "But you only met me today!" Jimi could see I didn't believe him, so he explained, "Yes, I know, but I feel that we've known each other for a long time. I've been searching all my life for you. Today I found you. I'm sure you're the one for me."

Slowly I realized that he was serious, and I became more and more nervous and bewildered. He asked me to go with him to London after his concert tour, so that we could spend some time together and I could get to know him better. I didn't know what to say as I had never met anyone who spoke so directly and so intensely to me. I tried to change the subject, but he asked me to think about it.

We talked for two hours, during which time my feelings for him changed dramatically into something I still didn't want to accept. Soon afterwards Jimi's tour and road manager, Gerry Stickles, announced that it was time for them to drive to Köln (Cologne) for some interviews and their next concert. Jimi asked me to go to Köln

with him, but I made an excuse and told him that I would come later. I was too confused, and felt that I needed some time to myself to think about the whole situation. Jimi asked if I would walk outside with him to the car, and he took hold of my hand as we went through the hotel lobby. I tried not to show it, but I was surprised. I had been brought up in a rather conservative way, and to walk hand in hand with someone publicly to me meant he had at least to be my boyfriend. Jimi holding my hand without asking certainly caught me off my guard.

I was shocked when, before they left, Jimi suddenly took me in his arms and kissed me. As he drove off I was left standing on the spot, completely dumbfounded. Within two hours he had managed to turn my life upside down, and afterwards it would never be the same again.

A few hours later I drove to Köln to meet Jimi, but asked the Baron to escort me: I felt more protected that way. Driving along, I was struck by a strange feeling, and I realized I had fallen in love with Jimi.

We met in his hotel room, and he held me in his arms and said he had been worried that I wouldn't come.

Soon afterwards we all left for the concert hall. When we arrived we were forced to run to the stage door, protected by some roadies, because a large crowd had gathered waiting for the group. For a moment I was pushed apart from Jimi, who was holding my hand, and it became frightening, but then he managed to pull me through to the stage-door entrance. Backstage, reporters and everyone

> **Within two hours he had managed to turn my life upside down, and afterwards it would never be the same again.**

else wanted to talk to Jimi and take pictures of him. I tried to hide away, but he made me sit next to him.

When it was time for Jimi to go on stage, he asked me to come and we walked there hand in hand. Just before his entrance he kissed me and refused to go on until I promised I wouldn't leave while he was giving the concert. From the very beginning of our relationship he seemed to sense if I didn't feel right about something, almost as if he were telepathic. And he was right: at that moment I had been thinking that it might be better for me to leave, before I became further involved.

While they performed, I was deeply moved by Jimi's guitar-playing. I remember also how impressed I was by Mitch's drumming. He was the best drummer I had seen so far, elegant and energetic at the same time, a perfect match for Jimi's style of playing. From what Jimi told me, he and Mitch never became really close friends, but on a musical level they always had a very good understanding.

When we left the concert hall we had to rush to the car because crowds of fans were waiting outside. Even as the chauffeur started the car three people were climbing on the roof, and many others were surging forward. The situation became rather frightening, and Gerry Stickles, worried about the safety of Jimi, Mitch and Noel, ordered the chauffeur to drive faster. When Jimi realized what was happening he ordered them to stop the car, but no one listened to him. Instead the driver accelerated, and the three fans fell off the roof, although they were not hurt. I looked at Jimi and could see that he was upset – he was quiet for some time. He was an extremely sensitive person who never wanted anyone to get hurt.

We went to a club at Noel's request, and they jammed for some time, Noel playing lead guitar and Jimi bass. Afterwards, we were enjoying a Chinese meal when an old flower-lady passed through the restaurant carrying a basket full of flowers. Jimi called her over, bought a bunch of red roses and handed them to me, whispering in my ear, "They're for you – a symbol of my love."

Again, his doing this so publicly made me feel embarrassed, but I must admit that I loved his gesture – one of many such to follow. All the time we were together he was loving, caring and very protective, which made me love him all the more.

From the restaurant we went to the hotel. I had told Jimi earlier that evening that I wasn't ready yet for a physical relationship. I was inexperienced, and, although I loved him, I needed more time before committing myself. He explained that he understood, and that the reason for his wanting to be with me was that he honestly wanted me to be his girl. The moment he had seen me, he said, he had fallen in love. We must have talked for hours, about many things, but mostly finding out more about each other.

He told me that he was born in Seattle, when his mother was only seventeen. She was not ready to take care of him, and his father, Al Hendrix, had been drafted into the army for three years. Jimi described how he was shifted from one relative to another. Then, when Al returned and Jimi was sent home, his parents had an on-off relationship for a few years. The main thing that Jimi remembered about this was hearing them arguing, partly

> Jimi called her over, bought a bunch of red roses and handed them to me, whispering in my ear, "They're for you — a symbol of my love."

because his mother, Lucille, would leave Jimi and his brother Leon unattended while Al was working. In the end Lucille left, and Jimi was taken care of mainly by his father – a responsibility Jimi would always remember and respect his father for. Various other family members, including Nora, his American Indian grandmother, took care of him at one time or another if necessary. Jimi never forgot the pain he felt at being shuttled from one family to the next. He told me that whenever he started to feel at home, and to love the people he was with, he had to leave them.

It was especially painful to Jimi that his mother had left him, although she still saw from time to time. She died when he was sixteen. At eighteen, facing the strong probability of being drafted, Jimi volunteered for the army. This allowed him to choose a particular section. He opted for the US Army 101st Airborne Division, whose Screaming Eagle insignia came to symbolize for Jimi the pride he wished his father to feel in his son's accomplishment. But to Jimi, just as important as fulfilling his military service obligation was his desire to pursue his music without further interruption.

Jimi told me that his first love of art had been for painting. Later he became more interested in music, getting his first guitar when he was twelve. A couple of years later he started playing with various groups in and around Seattle, until he joined the army. He later told me much more about his childhood, but a lot of this is either private or already widely known.

We both realized that neither of us had really had a normal childhood. He had been concentrating on his guitar, while I had been busy practising my skating, so neither of us had had much time to play with other kids. And yet we came from very different backgrounds: he was from a poor family, while mine was well off. He was playing in smoky clubs while I was taking ballet lessons and going to the opera and the theatre. But these differences were not important to us. What really mattered was our love for each other and the closeness in the way we were thinking. As Jimi said later, I was his other half, his other heart.

We spent most of the night talking and then just fell asleep; that was enough for us. The hotel was next to Köln's famous cathedral, so the following day after breakfast I wanted to show Jimi how beautiful it was inside. As we walked towards the imposing Gothic building, with its soaring twin towers, Jimi told me that the last time he had been in a church was in Seattle. At that time he had been kicked out because they said he wasn't dressed properly. To my regret, the same thing now happened again. Just as we entered the cathedral, a priest stopped us and ordered us to leave at once because Jimi's trousers, shirt and fringed leather jacket weren't considered proper dress.

I was upset and embarrassed and didn't know how to explain to Jimi, who couldn't understand German, what had been said. I tried to tell him and we left, but for a while he said nothing. Later he was to tell me in detail what "the Church" had become in his eyes.

Jimi explained that he felt the Church had knowledge and wisdom, but that this had to be given in the right way to the people. Much of what is said is right, but seems false. He thought that the Church concealed too much, had distanced itself from the people it wanted to reach, and was not

He told me that whenever he started to feel at home, and to love the people he was with, he had to leave them.

Jimi believed in himself and his inner faith in seeking a path to God.

going to church for a few times and getting thrown out of there because you have tennis shoes on with a blue and black suit...brown shirt...and then after politics tell you this hog wash about this and that, you know, you decide, well let me get my own thing together, you know, and so music is my, my scene. My whole life is based round it. So quite naturally it becomes to be even more than a religion. And so what I learn, through the experience of it I try to pass on to other people, you know, through our music, so it won't be so hard for them to go around. Like for instance all this violence, people running through the streets, you know. I can understand their point but like, uh, if they dig the sounds and let the spiritual...it's like church actually, you know...just like church, how you go to a gospel church, and we're trying to get the same thing through modern day music, you know." (Interview with Flip Wilson, *The Tonight Show*, NBC-TV, July 1969)

In Jimi's eyes the Church often put the institution before the message. He believed that much of what the Bible says is right, but that people often interpreted it the way they wanted to. Jimi felt that that was wrong, and said to me, "They should read the truth from it, and not whatever is convenient and by that change it around. The truth never does change!"

We had just been thrown out of the cathedral when, to make matters worse, as we were walking back to the hotel some old women we passed made nasty racial comments about Jimi and me. I was shocked. It was the first time ever that I had heard people speak in this way. Luckily Jimi didn't understand what they said, but with his sensitivity, he must have gathered from the tone of their voices what they meant.

(Later on, when Jimi and I were living in

effective in putting across the message of God to the people. The Church had to some extent lost its way. He said also that in all religions all over the world people are trying to say something different, whereas they should all look to the same light. Jimi believed in himself and his inner faith in seeking a path to God.

"It's a thing that, uh, it's, I don't know...after

England, we didn't really suffer any racial discrimination, although we did sometimes get very odd looks. Towards the end of the sixties the English were already becoming fairly tolerant about seeing mixed-race couples.)

When we were back at the hotel, sitting in the lobby, one of Jimi's fans sat down at our table. He stayed and chatted with Jimi for at least half an hour, and as I listened to their conversation I got a deeper impression of how caring and interested Jimi was in other people's thoughts and feelings. Even when he was exhausted and badly in need of a rest, he would still have this very strong natural interest in others.

I stayed with Jimi for another day, before he flew off to his next concert. We decided it would be best if we met again once the tour was over. Jimi felt he couldn't protect me properly should a potentially dangerous situation arise while he was busy touring. I had already noticed while I was with him that life on the road was pretty rough. Jimi had gone through this for years and knew, as any rock musician will confirm, that anything can happen at any time in and around concerts. The crowds were often wild and excited. People would get drunk or stoned, in some cases freaking out or becoming violent. Jimi was also worried about certain things that could happen behind the scenes – for example, drinks getting spiked – and wanted to avoid exposing me to such dangers. I understood, and promised him that I would join him in London as soon as his tour had finished. Until then we had content ourselves with telephoning each other as often as possible.

I could take on the world with Jimi by my side and with our love to support us.

My parents, especially my father, were not happy when they heard about Jimi and me. My father had nothing against Jimi personally, and did not object to the fact that he was of a different race. But he believed that other people were not so tolerant, fearing that they could and would be cruel to us. He was worried that this would make me unhappy, and he tried to explain how prejudiced the world could be. I was young and thought I knew best, so I disagreed, although I found out that he was partly right about some people's minds. What I was definitely sure about was that I could take on the world with Jimi by my side and with our love to support us.

So when I drove to London in February 1969 my father didn't know that I was going to meet Jimi. I had only confided in my mother.

I took a hotel room near Marble Arch. Jimi wanted to move in with me, but I felt that things were moving too fast, and he understood. When we were not together he stayed at the group's flat in Brook Street with some other people. We would go shopping and walk through Hyde Park. If we went to the cinema we usually missed the beginning of the film, slipping in when it was dark, and slipped out again before the lights came up. There were times when Jimi wanted to be left alone and not to be recognized and stared at by everyone.

Most of the time we stayed in the hotel room, where we were not disturbed, talking for hours about Jimi's music, the world around us and ourselves. It was then that he started telling me about his spiritual experiences and the way he looked at life and beyond. I was spellbound as I

He started telling me about his spiritual experiences and the way he looked at life and beyond.

a cry from one soul to its mate:

..... "please .... please help me. they're
trying to take me away ... .
for .... for a crime That
I just cant help ... A crime they
Say I committed to make people happy
Sad, indeffrent, deaf, climax, cry,
laugh, life, intertaintment ... "forget
your life and fancy, young slave
You Belong to us, Ha Ha Ha"....
Please Gold & Rose .... please
help me......."!

listened to him. He told me that he was hoping to play music with a clearer and spiritual message in each song.

One day when Jimi was writing a lyric, he asked if it would be all right to use my name in his songs. I explained that I felt our relationship was far too private for everyone to know about it, and if he wanted to write songs about me he must use another name. Jimi was very understanding, especially when he realized how shy I was about this. In the future he kept his promise, using other names, but letting me know when he wrote a song about me.

It was also at that time that I started to ask him questions about the meaning of some of his songs. For example, I had always been curious about what might be behind the title of his song "Third Stone From The Sun". Jimi asked if I could guess, and when I said I had no idea he explained that the third stone, as seen from the sun, was the planet earth, positioned third after Mercury and Venus.

Another song I asked him about was "One Rainy Wish", from his album *Axis: Bold As Love*, which had been released in 1967. As I had always particularly loved this song because of his tender romantic feeling, I was interested to know what went through Jimi's mind when he wrote it.

He revealed to me that for many years he had known deep inside that it was part of his destiny to find his soul mate, something he said was a very special thing that only rarely occurred. In "One Rainy Wish" he described a dream of his in which he saw the woman destined for him. As elsewhere in his lyrics, here Jimi plays with a double meaning

"Golden Rose", a spiritual metaphor for the ultimate love Jimi was searching for in his life.

of a word or phrase. On the one hand he uses the colours "Gold and Rose" to illustrate certain psychic emotions within his dream, together with "misty blue and lilac". However, the other concealed yet equally important and intended meaning of this phrase is "Golden Rose", a spiritual metaphor for the ultimate love Jimi was searching for in his life.

Maybe it is not easy for somebody without close knowledge of Jimi's world to catch these hidden meanings. In the handwriting shown opposite he briefly hints at this connection between his soul mate and "Gold and Rose". He believed strongly in the magical quality of the concept of man and

He believed strongly in the magical quality of the concept of man and woman, husband and wife in a spiritual sense.

woman, husband and wife in a spiritual sense. Once you had found your soul mate – Jimi called it his other half or other heart – these two halves combined would generate and activate much greater power and achievement than is ever possible for a single man or woman.

The middle part of the handwriting mirrors the agony and suffering Jimi felt at having constantly to serve the public's demands and being labelled with such an artificial and inadequate reputation.

Jimi had discovered that I did oil paintings, and when he saw photographs of them he urged me to give up my profession as an ice-skating instructor and concentrate on my painting. This would have meant quite a step for me. However, he really pushed me into becoming an artist, and in the end I had to promise him that I would do so, although I only agreed because of my feelings for him. I was far from confident of my abilities as a painter. For me, painting had been just a hobby, but Jimi seemed to see something more in my work, and started to make plans for our arts to be joined together in the near future.

He also told me about the stress and exhaustion he felt after two and a half years of constant touring all over Europe and America, plus recording on top of this. He said that he had needed a holiday for a long time, but that his manager, Mike Jeffery, kept on booking new tours, often without first informing him. He was therefore determined to take a holiday, after completing some recording and an American tour, around the end of May or the beginning of June. He asked me to look for a house near a lake in the Black Forest in Germany, and to rent it for four weeks, but to let no one know about it, so we would not be disturbed.

Jimi also made detailed plans to buy a house near Los Angeles, right on top of the hills, overlooking the sea, and asked me if I would like the interior decorated in the North American Indian style. I loved the idea, as I had always felt close to their culture. He even made plans to build a circular house with round rooms, perching on a cliff top, again close to Los Angeles and overlooking the sea below. He wanted the house to be circular, he explained, because nothing in the world of nature is square.

In the evening we often went to the Speakeasy, at that time the most fashionable club on the London music scene. Sometimes Baron von-der-Osten-Sacken, who was also in London at this time, would join us there. From time to time Jimi liked to jam with other musicians at the Speakeasy, and on a couple of occasions we went to the Brook

Street flat, where Jimi jammed with a congas-player called Rockie.

One day in March Jimi and I went into a jeweller's in the King's Road, Chelsea, where the day before I had bought myself a beautiful gold snake ring. Jimi had admired it, and told me he would like one too, so that we would both be wearing the same ring. After he had bought an identical one, he exchanged rings with me, saying, "I want them to be our engagement rings."

> He started to make plans
> for our arts to be joined...

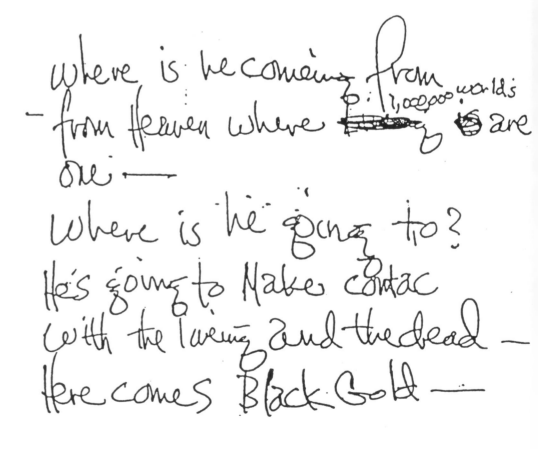

where is he comeing from
— from Heaven where ~~they~~ 1,000,000 worlds are
one —
where is he going to?
He's going to Make contac
with the living and the dead —
Here comes Black Gold —

I was very surprised and didn't know what to say. He explained that the snake is a magical symbol of wisdom and enlightenment which can be used to ward off evil. He said that if two people are joined together and they both wear a snake ring, it will unite them even more strongly. Through the symbol of the snake, the rings would, as he put it, "keep their promise." Naturally I felt happy, but also still overwhelmed at the speed with which our relationship was developing.

> He said that if two people are joined together and they both wear a snake ring, it will unite them even more strongly.

Later that evening we went to the Speakeasy and ate in the restaurant. Suddenly, in the middle of the meal, Jimi stood up, took me by the hand and led me from table to table, showing off the rings and announcing to people that we had just become engaged. This again took me completely by surprise, as I had never imagined that he would announce our engagement publicly, especially without warning me first. He told me later that he hadn't said anything before because he was sure that I would try to stop him. This was probably true, for I felt that I should have told my parents first. Later, when he was in America, Jimi also told people whom he trusted about our engagement, among them Juma Sultan, his percussionist.

Jimi wanted to meet my family at once, but I asked him to give me a little time to prepare my parents for the news of our engagement, and he agreed. A few days later I returned to Germany. I knew that my father would be shocked. He was a kind man, but also strict and conservative. It was going to take some convincing on my part to gain his consent. We were a close family and I really wanted my father to accept Jimi as one of us and to welcome him into the family. It took me some days to gather up enough courage to speak to my father about the subject. He was not at all happy, but in the end he agreed to meet Jimi.

Just as Jimi was preparing to fly to Düsseldorf, Mike Jeffery rang him and told him to come to New York immediately. Jimi told me that he would have to go, but that he would return in two or three days.

When Jimi arrived in New York his manager told him that Mitch and Noel were on their way to join him. He had booked studio time for the group to do some recording before starting their US tour. Jimi was very upset, as he had planned to fly back to Europe to meet my family, and he had a row with Jeffery. He also found out that his manager had added new dates to the tour, which would now last until the end of June. As had happened many times before, Mike Jeffery had ruined Jimi's plans for a badly needed holiday, to which we had both been looking forward.

> He felt it was high time to take control over his music and his life...to convey more spiritual messages.

When Jimi asked Jeffery to shorten the tour, he was told that the money was needed and also that if he broke the tour contract Jeffery had signed in his name, it would cost Jimi dearly. Once again, his manager had arranged things over Jimi's head, only informing him when it was too late to change the arrangements.

Jimi told me he was thinking of leaving his manager for good. He felt it was high time to take control over his music and his life, especially as he wanted to change his image and his music drastically, to convey more spiritual messages with solutions for the people and the problems in life. However, he feared Jeffery would do everything in his power to prevent this.

In the last eighteen months of his life, several threatening events made Jimi cautious. In May 1969 he was arrested at Toronto Airport for carrying drugs which he believed Jeffery had got someone else to plant on him. Death threats and other attempts to intimidate Jimi followed. He was even kidnapped by people who told him they were Mafiosi, then miraculously "rescued" on Jeffery's orders. These events made Jimi ask me not to join him in New York after his tour, as he feared that Jeffery might try to use me as a way of blackmailing Jimi. When I protested, saying that I could look after myself and that I wanted to help him, Jimi told me about a dream he had had some months before. He had made this into a song called "Look Over Yonder". In this dream he saw an evil force taking his love away after discovering her.

Jimi believed the dream to be a premonition – a warning about what could happen if his love was discovered – and he wanted to be able to protect me from its becoming reality.

He took his dreams very seriously. Billy Cox, the bass-player who replaced Noel Redding, remembered in an interview with *Guitar World* in September 1985, how on one occasion Jimi did not

Look over yonder

Well, he's talking to my babe

They found my peace pipe on her

Now they're dragging her away

Lord knows we don't need

A devil like him beating us around

Well, he's knocking on my door

Now my house is tumbling down.

turn up to a concert because he had a dream that the gig was cancelled. Jimi, to whom dreams could be very real, was sure the gig would not take place and went back to sleep.

Jimi didn't feel safe any more, and told me that he also felt unable to protect me from anything that might happen. He told me to wait for him, and that he would come as soon as he had sorted out everything with his manager. He wanted to break free from his management first and then join me in England.

She is real --- And this is beyond Heaven Itself") I must protect for the love of Happiness for my Mate to make reunion as One, we must not be late ----

Everything took so much longer than either of us had anticipated, but our love was the bridge that kept us united.

While we were apart Jimi wrote some poems for me. He sent this one in May 1969:

She put a welcome on the gate
Owns my soul this is my fate
Unfinished Love. I'm coming home
From here on in we won't be alone

Activity man – won't be late
For you my love I dedicate

Midnight magic deadline calling
Where hearts do feel and suffer
Chasing shadows of a living past
Giving my message, listen to the blast

Activity man – won't be late
For you my love I dedicate

Still blindfolded this time not afraid
A tired traveller so don't delay
Glow little lantern here over my way
Lead me, hold me and keep me today

Activity man – won't be late
For you my love I dedicate.

MONIKA AND JIMI IN EARLY 1969.

TUNNEL OF LIGHT

I always experienced the music that Jimi created as something very special, something that inspired and touched countless people all over the world. At its most inspirational it can almost draw you into a tunnel, taking you on an illuminated journey through space and time.

In this painting the guitar neck symbolizes the stairway to another world, another dimension, which is represented by the tunnel of light.

Many people have told me that they experienced the opening up of a new world within themselves when they listened to Jimi's music for the first time. His way of expressing himself musically touched, and is still touching, the human soul to its core. It seems to open a door into an unknown and mysterious world, overflowing with beauty and full of many wonders to discover. Yet this is the world as it is meant to be: positive, creative and spiritual, not ruled by materialistic values and illusions, but ruled by the laws of love.

To bring out the actuality of this other – and true – reality was Jimi's foremost goal. He frequently mentioned to me that he believed too many people are not awake, not their true selves, but just "functioning", shut away in their "plastic cages", as he put it. On the other hand, he was convinced that people could change the world, if they would realize the truth. He believed that in

order to solve the problems of our planet, people should become active themselves, instead of leaving it all to the ruling élite. So the message behind Jimi's work is not a hazy one. Rather it concerns each and every problem we face on this planet today.

Jimi was not a missionary, but a poet with a mission. He liked to spread his political message in a lyrically coded, symbolic way. So, for example, the song title "House Burning Down" represents not just one house, but also the whole world: a world in which the family of mankind is meant to be living as in one big house. Two world wars have shown what happens if brother fights brother, terrorizing and killing each other in the name of so-called higher values. Thus, the world was set on fire, and huge parts of the house were burnt down.

From the end of 1968 Jimi sometimes referred to his music as "Sky Church Music", emphasizing his conviction that music, especially of the right kind, could unite people by drawing them towards the spiritual world and God. Jimi did not believe in the institution of the Church, but he was a very religious person in a universal sense. So music to him – and he tried to explain this in some of his interviews – was a key to achieving a higher state of mind, a naturally higher state of being. As opposed to the artificial "high" evoked by drugs.

Jimi looked upon his music as a tool, a means of movement, both physical and psychic – a spaceship that he invited the listener to enter and fly off to other planets and galaxies, other thoughts and emotions.

In the painting the darkness around the tunnel of light represents the spiritual darkness of the society and world in which we live – a world which has lost its course, because so many people have lost their inner direction and are still asleep, untouched by the truth and purpose of their life.

The rainbow between Jimi and the tunnel of light symbolizes the bridge between our physical plane and the higher dimension of the tunnel. Jimi was fascinated by the symbol of the rainbow, as it had a special significance for him. Somehow the rainbow seemed to suit Jimi's nature, an expression of which was his imaginative and colourful way of dressing. But it was not only the rainbow's colours that attracted Jimi. To him, the rainbow was a magical and lyrical symbol, a metaphor for the all-uniting force behind the multiplicity of natural and spiritual phenomena. He used this powerful image a few times in his songs and once for his group Gypsy Sun & Rainbows. As it was unification that Jimi was trying to express and bring about, he himself, like the rainbow, can be seen as a messenger between the worlds.

"We plan for our sounds to go inside the soul of the person actually, y'know. And see if they can awaken some kind of thing in their minds, y'know, 'cause there's so many sleeping people."

THE DICK CAVETT SHOW, ABC-TV, AUGUST 1969

JIMI'S IMAGE – A STORY OF DISGUISE

Jimi was famous – or rather infamous – for burning his guitar on stage. Few people know that this happened very seldom – maybe on only three or four occasions. As I will explain later, this whole act was contrived, mainly to attract public attention.

Having learned from Jimi himself that his real aim was not to destroy guitars, but rather to wipe out all forms of hatred, corruption and discrimination, in this picture I show him symbolically burning these scourges of mankind.

Jimi was opposed to any form of lie or deceit. He knew that at the bottom of the world's worst problems lay the lack of will or inability of the individual to be honest and upright.

Taking part in building up a false image in the early stages of his career was probably Jimi's biggest mistake. It caused him a great deal of trouble and made him suffer many injustices. He soon realized with regret that ironically he himself had become a victim of a concealment of the truth to which he had not objected initially. From then on, he turned against this distortion and corruption of his public image, fighting hard to rectify the false picture.

In order to judge him properly, it is therefore important to know about the development and background of this side of Jimi. At the beginning of 1967, before Jimi became famous, his then manager, Chas Chandler, succeeded in getting him and the Experience on the Walker Brothers' farewell British tour. At the time, the Walker Brothers were sex symbols, even though they were in the process of splitting up.

Chandler calculated that Jimi could take over their mantle if everything was planned and carried out carefully. He explained later that they worked on developing the big, flamboyantly sexual stage act which was to give Jimi his reputation as a wild man and sex maniac. The plan was to use Jimi's natural talent for showmanship in order to attract attention by any means possible. When Chandler saw how the audience reacted and what an incredible amount of press coverage it generated, he realized they had hit the jackpot, and followed it up.

According to Chandler, and confirmed by Keith Altham, a music journalist, it was at the first Walker Brothers concert of the tour, in March 1967, that Altham came up with the idea of Jimi burning his guitar. A roadie was sent out to buy some lighter fuel which Jimi would spray over his guitar. Jimi's dramatic on-stage destruction of his instrument convinced both public and press that he was wild and outrageous, without their knowing the true story behind the act.

From then on, Chandler and later, Mike Jeffery, both kept feeding this fabricated image. Jimi told me that his managers and some record companies were even careful to choose which photos of him the press was allowed to print, so as not to endanger the concept they had created. They exercised much the same control over posters and LP covers. The whole process was skilfully planned and executed. Whatever seemed to suit their aim to make Jimi famous was right. In press releases they reduced Jimi's age by two years in order to attract a younger audience.

Lord my whole soul is so tired and aching Feel like I got ran over by public opinion in the past.

Spontaneous or incidental actions by Jimi were also integrated into the show. As Chandler remembers, "Jimi was pulled off stage by a few over-enthusiastic fans and as he jumped back on stage he threw his guitar on before him. When he picked it up he saw that it had cracked and several of the strings were broken – he just went barmy and smashed everything in sight. The German audience loved it and we decided to keep it in as a part of the act when there was a good Press about or when the occasion demanded it." (Keith Altham, *New Musical Express*, November 1968)

Jimi's original stage act was full of humour – he never wiggled his tongue without smiling like a little boy. He did not take such things seriously, which was a mistake, for many others did. They failed to catch the purely humorous note of it all, and Jimi played the game, unfortunately unaware of what would come from it.

Later Jimi told me that at first he went along with everything. His manager impressed on him that this was the only way to success, especially since he was a coloured person. He pointed out that no coloured or black man had ever broken through the barriers to join the inner circle of rock and roll.

A year later Jimi started to understand the devastating effect all this pretence had had on him as a musician. He started to worry more and more and to notice that people came to his concerts not to listen to his music but to watch the "wild man" on stage. He saw that people expected him to live up to his image, for at some of the later concerts some would boo him when he played calmly, without any wild actions. In his song "Midnight Lightning" Jimi expresses his feelings about this:

He asked, even pleaded with, his manager and the record company to show the real Jimi Hendrix and not the fabricated model they had created. Before the release of his double album *Electric Ladyland* Jimi had asked the record company in writing to design the cover according to his wishes. His letter included detailed sketches of how he wanted the outside and inside of the cover to look. He wished to use a photograph by Linda McCartney of Jimi, Mitch and Noel among children, sitting on the "Alice in Wonderland" statue in New York City's Central Park. In his letter Jimi emphasized that: "Any other drastic change from these directions would not be appropriate according to the music and our group's present stage." However, the album was released in Britain with a crowd of naked women on the cover, and had clearly been chosen to reinforce Jimi's lurid image. Once again he had been bypassed for purely business reasons, as it was this wild, sexy persona which his record company and manager believed the fans and press wanted and would sell records.

Mike Jeffery constantly strengthened this false image, doing his best to keep Jimi in line and not to let him rock the boat. One of the first such occurrences was in the summer of 1967, when Jeffery booked the Jimi Hendrix Experience on a nationwide US tour with the Monkees, a pop band who appealed to very young fans, many of them no more than nine years old. This episode says a lot about Jeffery's total lack of understanding of the true artistic side of Jimi's act. A less compatible combination of bands could hardly be imagined. And of course it didn't work out. However, when the Experience left the Monkees' tour, Jimi's manager and publicity team again knew how to make the most of the situation, once more carrying out their plans at Jimi's expense. A story was invented that outraged parents and a right-wing women's group, the Daughters of the American Revolution, had been shocked by Jimi's obscene performance and had demanded that he be taken off the tour. It was a skilfully manipulated story and predictably the press was not interested in learning about the true facts, for once again everything fitted in with Jimi's spectacular and profitable image.

Alarmed by this situation, from 1968 until his death in the autumn of 1970 Jimi was struggling to shake off his renegade image and establish himself as a serious musician and composer. One of his most famous quotes on this subject dates from the last year of his life:

"I don't want to be a clown any more. I don't want to be a rock and roll star."

(INTERVIEW WITH SHEILA WELLER, *ROLLING STONE*, NOVEMBER 1969)

Jimi explained to me that the main thing he wanted was for people to listen to his music. Music was an essential part of him, and the effect he wanted to have on his audience was to induce a state of awakening. His problem was that his music and his ideological integrity had been obscured by an all-powerful veneer of artificiality and disguise.

There can be few examples of artists whose public image and private persona have as little in common as in the case of Jimi Hendrix. In contrast to his official, rather uncivilized image, in private he was a very intelligent, gentle person, whose shyness was real. I soon realized there was a distinct division between Hendrix the star and Jimi the

person. It was then that I learned that one should never trust a publicly painted picture, but should rely on one's own judgement.

It was only a few weeks before his death that some journalists also began to realize this and to write about the real Jimi Hendrix and his gentle nature. In a series of interviews for the British press, Jimi spoke out in an unaccustomedly free manner, leaving a very favourable impression on those who conducted them. No longer was he called things like "The Wild Man of Borneo"; now it was "Gentleman Jimi".

Some of the articles published after his death also finally made an attempt to put the phenomenon of Jimi Hendrix into perspective. For example, Keith Altham wrote: "Jimi Hendrix is dead. I knew him. I liked him. I am sorry that he is dead...My first visit to the United States was with Jimi and the Experience for the Monterey Festival nearly four years ago and that revealed quite clearly the enormous contradiction between the person and the image he projected as a performer. On stage he was the demon savage – the wild man of the guitar to whom many of his public attributed a decadence and profanity which they suspected was the man himself. In reality he was quietly spoken, sensitive and nervous to an extent that he would emphasise the fact by constantly fluttering his fingers to his face and mouth in mock alarm." (*Record Mirror*, October 1970)

However, this reappraisal was not given enough time to take root, and when Jimi died the newspaper headlines again screamed, "JIMI HENDRIX DIES OF DRUG OVERDOSE", "DRUGS KILL JIMI HENDRIX" and so on. Other articles claimed he

went drugged-up to a sex party the night before he died.

Through the successful "work" of his manager and others, Jimi's true nature was kept concealed for many years to come. And even today, anybody trying to clarify the picture is forced to fight against all those who are interested in preserving the cliché and obscuring the truth.

"The establishment, they project a certain image and if it works, they have it made. They knock down somebody else for instance, you know, like saying I'm moody or so and so is evil or saying bla bla woof woof is a maniac or something, so that everybody gets scared to actually know about me. So that's part of the establishment's game." (Interview with Jane de Mendelssohn, *International Times*, March 1969

"The establishment, they project a certain image and if it works, they have it made."

Jimi was a traveller in space and time. Through his thoughts, dreams, visions and inspirations he was able to move between the dimensions. In many of his songs he was not only talking about the present, but also dealing with events of the past, as in "Up From The Skies" and "Belly Button Window", and the future, as in "Valleys Of Neptune – Arising" or "1983...(A Merman I Should Turn To Be)".

Jimi seemed to have the ability to switch from one time dimension to the next. He often spoke of ancient worlds and civilizations as if he had mental contact with them. His mind and spirit were free to travel through time and space and to behold ancient cultures and other planets, both in our universe and beyond it.

It was this concept that I have tried to express in this painting. Jimi is playing, his mind a million miles away, perhaps travelling within a huge galaxy, swirling around in the distance: one of the many galaxies full of life and mysteries waiting to be discovered.

Jimi seemed to have the ability to switch from one time dimension to the next.

PEACE

One of Jimi's most important messages was that our planet above all needs peace if mankind is to stand a chance of survival. In many of his songs – for example "Machine Gun", "House Burning Down" and "I Don't Live Today" – he showed what happens when one human being tries to gain power over another.

This painting shows Jimi under a corona of cosmic energy, playing his guitar for world peace. Three doves, ancient symbols of peace, hover above his head in emulation of his gesture of peace, inspiring and encouraging him to continue in his mission. These three emissaries represent symbolically peace for the earth, the Milky Way and the universe.

Jimi felt the need to rearrange and change our world into a different kind of place, in which it would be altogether more meaningful and worthwhile to live: a place where people, families, cities, nations and continents are finally permitted to live together in harmony, as was intended from the beginning of time.

However, he also knew that world peace could only spring from the will and ability of each individual to create his or her own personal peace. So, to him, peace meant more than just a lack of political aggression: it meant a state of mind and consciousness which enables us to transform our aggressive instincts into a source of positive and creative energy.

Jimi believed that wars were created by man and were not a product of fate. Most military conflicts were caused by irresponsible leaders whose prime motivations were greed and a hunger for power. In this respect nothing has really altered since the time of the Vietnam war, despite fundamental changes in the world. The theatre of war may have shifted its location, but the causes remain the same. All over the world young people, little more than children, are being sent to fight in wars which could have been avoided. As Jimi was convinced that all people are brothers and sisters in the deepest sense, he found the idea of brother fighting brother deeply offensive.

In "Machine Gun" Jimi recreated the whole apocalyptic atmosphere of warfare, giving us in the most effective terms a potent anti-war sound-painting.

Although the ultimate victims of war are people, Jimi knew that one could not ignore the responsibility of the individual. The people themselves, especially the young, need to scrutinize the facts, understand the state of the world and then endeavour to change it. He was convinced that changes could realistically be achieved, if the young and young-minded people wanted them. These changes would enable us and our children to live in a better world. In a tape-recorded interview with Nancy Carter in June 1969, Jimi said: "…there are a whole lot of people here who need that one little push, to tell them what they're here for… That's what I am in the world for…"

Yet Jimi believed that changes in the world are meaningless if we have not undergone a spiritual transformation. The revolution he had in mind was not purely a political one, but a spiritual one, eventually leading to more social and political justice. At the beginning of his career Jimi certainly dealt with his growing political and cultural influence – especially on the young – in an intuitive way. But he gradually became more aware and critical of his responsibility and influence, and attempted to handle it in an increasingly sensible and careful way.

Furthermore, as he often told me, he understood that, according to the law of Karma, violence only produces violence, unleashing a fatal and endless spiral of destruction.

Jimi had great admiration for Martin Luther King and the way he had made important advances for the black cause by peaceful methods. I remember that he spoke of King as someone very special. He rated him as a leading figure of world

"All music to me is pilgrimage to peace."

importance and closely followed his activities on behalf of human rights. Jimi himself stood up for the civil rights movement. His father told me about an incident that occurred when Jimi was still a backing musician. He and the group he played with at that time went into a cinema and sat in seats reserved for whites, to protest for equal rights for black and white. They were all arrested and put in jail until the owner of the club they played at came and bailed them out.

Therefore Jimi was devastated by the news of Martin Luther King's assassination. Yet he knew deep in his heart that the bullet which killed King was unable to kill the peace movement he had called into being. And the future proved Jimi to be right.

The day after King was shot, the Experience were scheduled to perform in the largely black community of Newark, New Jersey. There were fears that there could be riots throughout the city and before the show large crowds had gathered near the concert hall. To diffuse tensions, the authorities recommended that the group make their way across the city and go ahead with the concert.

As he walked on stage, Jimi said, "This number is for a friend of mine." According to the eyewitness account of Mark Boyle, a member of Soft Machine's crew: "He abandoned completely his normal set. The band played an improvisation which was absolutely hauntingly beautiful. Immediately everyone knew what this was about. This was a lament for Martin Luther King. And within minutes the whole audience was weeping… The music had a kind of appalling beauty. Harrowing music. When he came to the end there was no applause, he just put down his guitar, the whole audience was sobbing, and he just walked quietly off the stage." (*The South Bank Show*, London Weekend Television, October 1989)

As soon as Jimi became famous, the radical political grouping known as the Black Panthers tried to recruit him, to make him contribute to party funds and to otherwise use him for their own purposes. Jimi was by nature an open-minded person: he always wanted to hear both sides of an argument before judging what he felt was the right thing to do. So he listened to them and debated with them, trying to understand what they were preaching. "There's certain people on this earth that have the power to do different things, for instance in the Black Power Movement they're using it wrongly." (Interview with Jane de Mendelssohn, *International Times*, March 1969)

Jimi's political beliefs and those of the Black Panthers were miles apart. Although he was not a pacifist in the strictest sense – he believed that some evils just cannot be met with passive suffering – he was nevertheless strongly opposed to violence. By contrast, the Black Panthers advocated the use of force for political means, and Jimi was unable to support this view.

Jimi had only just begun to spread his political creed through his songs and interviews: he had so much more still to do. However, we can all help his and Martin Luther King's dreams to be fulfilled by forgetting what separates one human being from another and concentrating on what it is that we all have in common that unites mankind.

well I see black and white and red and yellow even green — getting to gether And thier weapons are shineing clean - But I'm not talking about swords, knives, and guns - I'm talking about the power of God and the new Riseing Sun

VOODOO CHILD

Listening to Jimi's music can be a very magical experience. To me, it appears different and new every time I encounter it. It never leaves me untouched. Sometimes it just flows along like a river, soothing and peaceful. At other times it seems to erupt with the sheer force of a volcano. This painting is intended to illustrate metaphorically this eruptive side of Jimi's artistic temperament and the magic behind it.

On one occasion I spoke to Jimi about his songs "Voodoo Chile" and "Voodoo Child (slight return)". I asked him why he called himself a "voodoo child", because for me voodoo had always meant something to do with black magic. He explained that the word came from Africa, and just meant magic in general, and that originally voodoo was a religion in which magic is used, as it is in many other religions. Depending on the purpose for which this magic is used, it can be positive or negative. Voodoo was meant to be a positive force.

Jimi believed the pure, positive magic belongs to the human race and is a link to the Creator. Religion and magic come from the same source in the universe, but the two have become separated, as both have been misused so often by the negative forces. All the good things can be abused – a stone may be used by one person to build a house, while another might use it to kill his fellow man. Yet the stone remains the same – everything depends on how it is used. And so it is with magic.

Jimi had great faith in the Higher Powers and sought spiritual answers within himself. His music and the spiritual awakening it promoted made him realize that music was also a way towards a higher way of thinking and could become a spiritual path towards God. He said he found his own personal religion within himself, and called it "Sky Church Music". He felt the need for people to experience spiritual growth. Jimi talked in detail about positive magic like healing and believed that everyone possesses these magical powers.

When Jimi explained the meaning of "Voodoo Chile" and "Voodoo Child (slight return)" it became clear to me that he was talking about positive magic. So he did not practise negative magic, nor did he have anything to do with voodoo in the conventional sense.

Jimi had a rare ability to draw powers from natural as well as spiritual sources and to channel those energies into a constant flow of inspiration. This was one of the reasons why he loved to jam with other musicians so much – to create a flow of energy he could tune in to, almost a stream of consciousness that could later be used as a basis for sounds, musical pictures and ideas in general.

Many of those who have experienced Jimi playing live have remarked on the impressive force of his guitar work and the charisma he projected both on and off stage. Some of his concerts felt almost like magical ceremonies, with Jimi trying to invoke as much positive power as possible in order to share it with his audience. I know that many of those who attended these special concerts found them to be higher experiences, difficult to express in words.

In my painting Jimi stands calm, but concentrating deeply, while the volcano blazes around him like a wing of fire. This is meant to illustrate the principle that all great achievement, revolution or renewal can only come from calm concentration on one point.

Jimi, who was normally such a creative and active person, also sometimes liked to calm down and just think or meditate. It is this dual aspect of his character that I experience in Jimi's music – the blend of calm, lyrical intensity with loud, forceful expressiveness. The first aspect could be seen when Jimi just closed his eyes and played calmly, almost for himself, perhaps a song like "Little Wing". The second could be seen in the Jimi of extrovert outfits and flamboyant showmanship, who screamed "Foxy Lady" into the microphone and teased his audience with mischievous gestures. This was the side in which the public showed the most interest.

Jimi

had

great

faith

in the

Higher

Powers

and

sought

spiritual

answers

within

himself.

PURPLE

HAZE –

JESUS

SAVES

E ver since "Purple Haze" was released in 1967, many people have been – and still are – convinced that Jimi was writing about drug experiences and that this was the real and full meaning of the song. ("Purple hearts" were amphetamine tablets, a popular drug of the time.)

This is not correct. Jimi explained to me that when he wrote the lyric to "Purple Haze" its original title was "Purple Haze – Jesus Saves" and that it was a song about a dream he had. In this dream he looked down on earth and saw an unborn foetus waiting for its birth as if it were pointing at the time for it to be born. At the same time he saw spirits of the dead leaving earth. Later in the dream he went on a journey through the dimensions, and was walking under the sea. Part of the song was

about the purple haze which surrounded him, engulfed him, and in which he got lost. He told me later what a traumatic experience this had been, but that in the dream his faith in Jesus had saved him.

Before the single of the song had even been released, Jimi stated: "I dreamt a lot and I put a lot of my dreams down as songs. I wrote one called 'First Look Around The Corner' and another called 'The Purple Haze', which was all about a dream I had that I was walking under the sea." (Interview with John King, *New Musical Express*, January 1967) The original lyric was a few pages long but Jimi was told by his management to cut it short as at that time single recorded songs were supposed to be no more than about three minutes long. So most of the original words never appeared on record.

In a tape-recorded interview, obviously moved, Jimi says: "You know the song that we had named 'Purple Haze'? That was about a...it had about a thousand thousand words, and it didn't...Ooooh it gets me so mad 'cause that isn't even 'Purple Haze', you know...You should have heard it, man. I had it written out. It was about goin' through all these...through this land, you know. This mythical...because that's what I like to do is write a lot of mythical scenes." (Interview with Meatball Fulton, December 1967)

And later, in 1969, he said: "Most of the songs, like 'Purple Haze' and 'Wind Cries Mary', were about ten pages long but then we're restricted to a certain time limit so I had to break them all down, so once I'd broken the songs down I didn't know whether they were going to be understood or not. Maybe some of the meanings got lost by breaking them down, which I never do anymore, it's such a

> "I dreamt a lot and I put a lot of my dream down as songs."

— Throw all that MIXED UP
away — All that
Speed — dirt is gonna clog and
hurt —

"Purple Haze" is not a song about drugs...

drag." (Interview with Jane de Mendelssohn, *International Times*, March 1969)

"Purple Haze" is not a song about drugs, because Jimi explained the meaning to me. Then over the years I repeatedly tried to correct people's preconceptions and false ideas. Few people seemed to want to know the truth, and "Purple Haze" could have gone down in history as a drug song had it not been for the fact that the first page of Jimi's original handwritten lyric came up for auction at Sotheby's in New York in 1990, and was consequently reproduced in the auction catalogue.

It was not only during his lifetime that people said Jimi took drugs. When he died the majority of the world's newspapers claimed he had died of a drug overdose. Both assumptions are incorrect.

In the late sixties drugs were looked upon in quite a different way from today, and had not nearly so heavy an image. Junkies and hard-drug users were around, but drugs had not yet grown into the massive problem they are today. In those days drugs were regarded as a part of a new cultural movement – almost a fashion – and many believed they could expand your mind.

Like many other musicians and young people at the time, Jimi experimented with drugs. He smoked hashish to help him relax, considering it less harmful than alcohol. He later tried LSD, although not before the Monterey Festival in June 1967, which was in fact six months after "Purple Haze" was written. He soon realized that drugs only led to a certain artificial high which did not last. He often explained that, by means of music, one can achieve a "natural high" which is limitless, reaching a state of mind that goes far beyond the

effect of any drug. Always open to the spiritual dimension, Jimi frequently achieved such a natural high.

His reason for using drugs was not so much to "space out" and forget everything, as to mirror and expand the spiritual side of his personality, which was already very strongly developed. Claire Moriece, cook for Jimi and his band at the Woodstock house, comments: "Having started working with Jimi and getting to know him better, I was very surprised to see how different he was from what I had imagined: humble and funny. As a true messenger and medium, Jimi was tuned into a spiritual place where I believe he connected to the great truth of the Universe.

"In regards to drugs the stigma of him as an addict is false. Jimi's perception was experimental – he didn't use them as part of an everyday habit. In Jimi's mind-set drugs were more like semi-conductors than they were an escape. In those days drugs were seen as a means to expand your mind and spirituality. I can only say he really was a

he would accept and put the drugs in his pocket, only to throw them away later.

The same thing happened the night before he died, when I picked him up from a party. When he came out of the house he opened his hand and in it were at least six kinds of pills and other drugs. I asked him if he had taken any, and he said no and dropped them down a drain in the street.

It is confirmed by people who were close to him that Jimi never took heroin or other hard drugs. Eric Barrett, one of his road managers, said: "All the years I was with him I never saw a needle at any time. Sure, he smoked pot or he'd take an upper. But he wasn't a junkie. I never saw him do anything serious. At times he was taking acid, but it wasn't like a daily event." (*Hendrix*, Chris Welch, 1972)

Jimi would only smoke a joint when playing a concert or recording at the studio, which is where he spent most of his time. Eddie Kramer, his sound engineer for most of his years in the limelight, said that he never saw him take any drugs, apart from a

"...what I like to do is write a lot of mythical scenes."

deeply spiritual and wonderful person."

Jimi soon recognized the dangers of drug-taking, especially as he saw more and more musicians and others around him unable to handle their drug consumption, many getting hooked and losing control of their lives.

As a famous figure Jimi was constantly offered drugs by fans or other people, and he was not very good at saying no. He didn't want any kind of barrier between himself and his fans, which made it fairly easy for anyone to contact him. I saw people giving Jimi drugs as a present, thinking it would please him, and, as he didn't want to offend them,

joint when he was recording day and night.

In fact, Jimi was unable to play his guitar if he took any other, heavier drugs. This became clear at a benefit concert at New York's Madison Square Garden in January 1970. Although Mike Jeffery, his manager, opposed it, Jimi wanted to play benefit concerts, and he was really looking forward to this gig. However, he told me later that before the concert began, someone (he thought it was either his manager or a girl he knew) spiked his drink with a hallucinogenic drug. When he went on, the drug was already beginning to affect him, and he was only capable of playing a couple of songs

Purple Haze
— Jesus Saves

Purple Haze...Beyond insane
Is it pleasure or is it
pain —
Down On the ~~see~~ ~~red~~ ceiling
looking up at the
~~Bed~~ See my Body painted
Blue and red —

I see fetus un borns
~~Why is Everybody~~
pointing at the Time
Rush through Space...
My Hair is Blowing in thier minds
~~~~ through the Haze
I see 1,000 crosses
Scratched in the

He regarded taking drugs, drinking alcohol, even smoking cigarettes, as weaknesses and nothing to be proud of.

before having to leave the stage. He left the arena alone and very upset, especially because he had disappointed his fans.

Another incident that really shook Jimi up was when he was arrested at Toronto Airport in May 1969 for possession of hash and heroin. To his surprise, the drugs were found in his flight bag. Jimi told me he was sure someone had planted the stuff there. He again believed that Jeffery was responsible.

The trial was set for December and the months leading up to it were a traumatic period for Jimi. He knew he could face up to seven years in prison if convicted. The enormous pressure was only lifted when he was found not guilty after a witness stepped forward in his defence, stating that she had seen someone put something in Jimi's flight bag at the time.

Eric Barrett recollects: "He was busted in Toronto for heroin and was completely upset. He thought he'd go down for ten years and it wasn't even his smack. Some chick had thrown it in his bag. He wasn't feeling well when he left to go to the airport. He said he had a headache and the chick said, 'This will help the headache.' He never checked his bag." (*Hendrix*, Chris Welch, 1972)

I know from Jimi himself that there were people around him, including his manager, who were vitally interested in keeping him supplied with drugs and who offered them to him all the time. They obviously believed that it would make it easier to handle and control him this way,

especially if they could get him addicted (a common method of dealing with rock musicians). Luckily it never got that far with Jimi, because he wouldn't allow it to happen. It was also his manager – plus the media – who were responsible for promoting Jimi's reputation as a big drug user. The basic premise was clear and simple: "clean" rock stars don't sell product.

Likewise untrue is the allegation that Jimi died of a drug overdose. When he died in September 1970 he had no drugs in his system apart from some sleeping pills and traces of amphetamine. There was absolutely no trace of hard drugs. Corroborating Eric Barrett's statement quoted above, the pathologist found no needle marks on Jimi's body. (The needle marks of a heroin user never disappear.) He did not even die as a result of taking too many sleeping pills, for there were not enough in his system to kill him. The cause of death was suffocation through inhalation of vomit, although the medical reason why this happened is still unclear.

Unfortunately, before the inquest on Jimi's death, I was forbidden by the authorities to make a statement in public for ten days, which gave the press the opportunity to publish whatever they wanted. This led to all the wrong or half-correct coverage after his death.

A press conference at which I could explain the true circumstances of Jimi's death was scheduled for the day of the inquest, but cancelled by Jeffery, again, in retrospect, for obvious reasons. He was simply not interested in clearing up the public misconception that Jimi had died of a drug overdose. Even after Jimi's death Jeffery was unwilling to interfere with his spectacular and lucrative reputation as a drug addict and eventual

drug victim. One tends to forget that with rock stars big business doesn't come to an end after the source of income has disappeared. On the contrary, in Jimi's case the sums of money mounting up year after year to this day are enormous.

Of course Jimi was not a saint. But I know, and he told me, that he regarded taking drugs, drinking alcohol, even smoking cigarettes, as weaknesses and nothing to be proud of. So it is wrong to keep on mentioning him in the same breath as rock stars who really were junkies. He was never addicted in such a desperate, helpless way, but in this area he was also – although it may sound strange – a seeker and explorer.

In 1990 Mitch Mitchell, Jimi's drummer for several years, explained: "Contrary to what some people have said, Jimi was never a junkie... Drugs were certainly consumed in those days by bands on the road, mainly the same drugs used by millions of housewives and businessmen. They did become a way of life. Even if you tried to avoid drugs yourself some asshole would come along and spike your drink."

Jimi therefore should be seen less in the role of a victim where drugs are concerned. In contrast to the classic drug user, his main motivation and interest lay not so much in repressing problems or psychological troubles as in finding and creating new ways and experiences. So, in my opinion, if Jimi is to be called a drug addict, then everyone who drinks alcohol should be called an alcoholic.

In any case, drugs were not essential for him to create music. It is known that his first album, *Are You Experienced*, was not made under the influence of drugs or alcohol, although the music of this early period was certainly his wildest and most freaky. Although the record appears to be the most drug-influenced of them all, in fact it sprang from Jimi's strong imaginative powers. These were the inspirational source he drew on – not drugs.

It is always misleading to try to categorize Jimi too rigidly. He was not interested in keeping the status quo but in expanding and developing, allowing himself to flow and grow with increasing experience. And as in so many areas, his attitude to drugs went through a process of development, changing and refining over the years. "I have outgrown these things," he would say. So if in the beginning he was somewhat naive and careless, he later came more and more to realize and face his responsibilities to himself and as a public figure.

In 1969 and 1970 Jimi repeatedly spoke out against drugs in interviews, as well as in some of his songs, for example in "Earth Blues": "Don't get too stoned, remember you're a man." In late August 1970 he told *Melody Maker*'s Roy Hollingworth:

"You know the drug scene came to a big head. It was opening up things in people's minds, giving them things that they just couldn't handle. Well music can do that, you know, and you don't need any drugs."

BUDDHA'S BLESSING

In August 1970, when Jimi had returned to England from his American tour, we were discussing some ideas for oil paintings that he wanted me to do. He asked me to paint a picture of Buddha and himself, with Buddha blessing Jimi. Only ten years after Jimi's death did I have enough confidence in my artistic abilities to fulfil his wish.

In this painting I tried to capture the peace and love emanating from Buddha within the surroundings of a beautiful Japanese garden. The tranquillity of a lake and a small waterfall supplies healing powers to mind and body. The blessing is symbolized by a golden ray of light coming from Buddha's "third eye" towards Jimi's forehead. A rainbow is arcing above them, symbolizing the bridge between heaven and earth. Jimi never saw this painting, but I hope I have done justice to what he had in mind. When I asked him why he wanted me to paint this particular picture, he replied that Buddha was the "Enlightened One" and that he felt close to him.

He explained that Buddha had been born as a prince, blessed with all worldly goods. However, when he became aware of all the misery in the world, he was seized by compassion and sacrificed his princely life, leaving home to search for the Truth and the solution to the problem of human suffering.

For years he kept searching and struggling. At one point, like Jesus, he was tempted by evil to leave the path of Truth. However, he did not succumb. Finally he reached the state of Enlightenment and continued teaching the knowledge he had gained until he died.

Jimi told me that he believed Buddha had found a way to show people the path to God. I have not studied Buddhism in detail, but I know that Jimi believed in at least two of its main principles. One was reincarnation. Jimi explained to me that he was sure that when a person dies only his body expires. The released spirit leaves the body to return to the Spiritworld and comes back at a later stage to be reincarnated – that is, reborn in another body on earth. Jimi believed that each soul has the possibility of evolving through the ages, growing in wisdom, love and strength, developing into a better, more enlightened being. He looked upon reincarnation as a challenge, seeing this world as a school, a place full of temptation and material obstacles which have to be overcome.

To become reincarnated as human beings means learning and developing until we have reached a certain point of evolution and eventually do not need to return to earth any more. The purpose of an individual's coming into the world can also be to help mankind by fulfilling a certain mission.

Another belief which Jimi shared to a degree with Buddha is the Law of Karma. At first I had no idea what he meant by this term. However, he explained that the Law of Karma was the Law of Life – not the tiny part of justice we see here on earth, but the Supreme Justice of the Cosmos. Only by understanding the Law of Karma can we assess and understand many of the injustices and cruelties which are poisoning the world. Karma is the executor of the Divine Cosmic Law.

When I asked Jimi how this principle worked, he gave me the example of a person doing something evil to someone else, and getting away with it in one life, only to have to suffer an equally heavy fate in one of his subsequent lives. The rule of Karma is as simple as it is efficient: you will always get back what you give. If you give love, you will receive love. If you destroy, you will suffer destruction yourself. Whatever you do, it will one day come back to you. You can't escape Karma – no one can – because it's the Divine Law.

Each soul has the possibility of evolving through the ages, growing in wisdom, love and strength, developing into a better, more enlightened being.

50

I Am You

This is a very private painting of Jimi and me. When he had finished writing his last poem, "The Story of Life", he gave it to me, telling me to keep it as a poem about us. Three words inspired me to do this painting: "I Am You".

I tried to catch the meaning of these words in this picture – not only indicating that Jimi and I had a special relationship but also looking at the idea in a more general way. Jimi believed, and I share his belief, that all people are one in a higher sense, and that everyone is capable of finding himself in any other person, especially so when two people are a predestined pair.

While I am sitting by a lake, looking into the water, I am reflected by Jimi's image on the surface. At the same time the castle in the background, the trees and the sky are also mirrored in the surface of the lake, which is covered by swathes of waterlilies. Have you ever noticed the visual depth and clarity of such a reflected image, when clouds can become flowing mountain landscapes and branches of trees turn into glistening waterfalls? The image may be more fragile and less "solid" than our normal world, but it is definitely more beautiful and mysterious. And though the image becomes blurred and dissolves once we try to touch it, it may yet be even more real than its physical counterpart.

Jimi kept saying to me that we should

understand "both sides of the sky". To me this means that we should live our lives on earth, but also be open to what we cannot touch or perceive with our physical senses – not restricting ourselves to one side, but striving to become complete human beings. Only by allowing ourselves to look into other worlds, I feel, can we get to the basis of our existence and develop.

The idyllic, fairy-tale setting of the painting reflects my feelings when I was with Jimi. It was more than happiness: my whole world was filled with new life and love – almost like in a fairy story, although not unreal, just real in a different sense. And I have always believed in the special truth behind fairy tales, just as I believe in images on water.

52

GENTLEMAN JIMI

After Jimi's death Bob Dawbarn wrote: "The point is that in all obituaries I just don't recognize the Hendrix I met. Granted, each man can be all things to all people, but I didn't find Jimi in the burblings of the gutter Sundays, nor in that incredibly embarrassing, so-called tribute by Eric Burdon on television… The first time I met Jimi, after seeing his stage act, I was expecting some sort of evil, monosyllabic monster. Instead I found a man of quite remarkable charm, an almost old-world courtesy and quite overpowering personality. He was one of those rare people – and they are much rarer in the supposedly glamorous world of popular music than you might think – who only had to walk into a room for his personality to completely envelop you." (*Sounds*, October 1970)

From my own experience, I can only support this assessment of Jimi's character. Every sensitive person who met him must have noticed the remarkable difference between his public image and his true nature. The real Jimi was completely different from the way he was depicted by the media.

Even at the height of his success he remained a humble, almost insecure person – one who was not selfish and cared more for others and the world than himself. He wanted people to share everything.

When he was looked on as a star, he still believed that he hadn't made it. He told me that for himself he was not satisfied at all, being only at the beginning of what he felt he had to do, and that there was still so much to be done.

So fame and success did not change him. On the contrary, he felt he was really lucky and several times expressed his gratitude. Even a few days before his death, when a fan approached us in a shop in London for Jimi's autograph, he was very happy to give his signature – almost as happy as the fan was to receive it.

Jimi worried about other people's feelings. He became aware that Noel Redding, who had been a lead guitarist before he joined Jimi's band, was unhappy playing bass guitar. So while they were touring Jimi started to look out for opportunities to jam in clubs after their concerts, where Noel could play lead and Jimi bass.

This happened when I was with Jimi in Köln in January 1969, while the Experience were touring Europe. After their concert in the city's Sporthalle, we went to a small club which Noel knew of. When the band had finished playing their set, Jimi asked if Noel, Mitch and he could use their equipment. It was strange to see that set-up, with Noel and Jimi swapping roles. They sounded just like any other group: their music had lost all its magic without Jimi on lead guitar.

Jimi couldn't stand the idea of hurting other people's feelings, and always tried to get the press to take as much notice of Noel, Mitch and other musicians he later worked with as they did of him.

There is an amusing story which illustrates very well this side of Jimi. One day while he was in New York, he took a taxi down to his recording studio. When the driver realized who his passenger was, he told Jimi that he himself was a good bassist,

and asked if he could come round to the studio after his shift and play with Jimi. Taking the cabbie at his word that he was a good musician, Jimi agreed. Sure enough, the man turned up with his instrument and started to jam with Jimi. He was hopeless. But Jimi didn't have the heart to hurt the feelings of this guy, who really believed he could play. The result was that they played together for hours, wasting Jimi's time and money, and all because Jimi was too kind-hearted to ask him to leave.

Jimi was a very sensitive person, and I soon discovered that he could pick up other people's feelings quite easily. However, this strong sensitivity, which was an asset to him as an artist, also made him quite vulnerable. I learned from what he told me that he had been hurt badly at various times in his life. Somehow he seemed to feel personal pain more strongly than most people.

talking about it and he explained that when he was first approached about the project, he had been told that it would be a positive and spiritual film. But when he later arrived in Maui, Hawaii, where it was to be shot, he found the script had been changed from how it had originally been described to him.

Jimi was still very upset when he told me about the script revision and said that because of it he had wanted to leave Maui at once. However, he was stopped and told that if he refused to participate he could be sued for breach of contract, which would cost him a great deal of money. Jimi felt that it was almost a threat, especially when he found out that Mike Jeffery, his manager, had more of a say in the film than anyone had previously cared to mention. Once the film had been released, Jimi intended to distance himself from it, so as to be free to explain what had happened. After he told me this story, he added that there had been many

I'll come back and buy this town, and put it

Many people took advantage of his kindness, especially when they realized they could get away with it. For instance, people would sit down at our table uninvited, dining at Jimi's expense without asking or even saying thank you when they left. It was strange to see that Jimi was aware of this yet didn't seem to mind. Jimi had an unshakeable belief that there was a good core in everyone, forgiving those who hurt him. There was a strange but beautiful innocence in him.

However, his concern for others and his willingness to trust sometimes led him into situations he didn't bargain for. One such incident occurred in the summer of 1970, after he had agreed to take part in a film which was later called *Rainbow Bridge*. A month later Jimi and I were

similar situations, where he had gone in expecting one thing, only to find quite another.

There was yet another twist to the story, for after Jimi's death Jeffery had the film re-edited in order to exaggerate Jimi's role way beyond anything he had been led to believe.

Money meant nothing to Jimi. He needed it to survive from day to day, and to be able to do what he wanted to do artistically, but he was not in any way materialistic. His attitude towards money was one of complete detachment. As he told Meatball Fulton in a taped interview in December 1967: "The money doesn't make any difference to me, yeah, 'cause that's what I make the money for is to make better things, you know, happen. I don't have no value on money at all."

"The money doesn't make any difference to me, yeah, 'cause that's what I make the money for is to make better things, you know, happen. I don't have no value on money at all."

If Jimi had money he would spend it, mainly on new equipment or to help other people. For instance, if he met a young musician without a guitar, Jimi would go out and buy him one, remembering the days when he had no instrument of his own and his father and later a girlfriend in New York bought him one.

Anyone who knew Jimi could count on his help. As soon as he received any money he would send some to his father and his family as he knew they needed it. Whatever Jimi did, it was not for financial gain, but because at the time he felt it was right.

Money meant so little to him that even at the height of his success he didn't mind not having much of it. When I first met Jimi, at the beginning

Although he appeared quite a nervous person, always rather restless, Jimi had a great sense of humour. He could make you roll around in fits of laughter and was wonderful at impersonating people. He would have made a marvellous actor. A little-boy grin would appear on his face when, completely out of the blue, he said something really funny. Sometimes he pretended to be someone else, slightly exaggerating that person's characteristics, like a true comedian. He did it in a very subtle way, through his expression, his eyes looking up or rolling around, or just in the way he would slightly overemphasize a word.

Jimi's humour came through in some of his songs – for example, "Hear My Train A-Comin'". He often changed the lyrics of his songs, and in one version of this number he says, "I'll come back and buy this town, and put it in my shoe, I might even give a piece to you." Jimi always kept a little

in my shoe, I might even give a piece to you.

of 1969, I noticed that if he needed change, say to pay for a meal, he had to go to Gerry Stickles, his tour and road manager, and ask for some. This seemed strange to me, and when I asked Jimi if he had his own bank account he told me that Jeffery was putting all his money into a special account in Jimi's name, for his future use.

A few months later Jimi discovered that the money he had earned had mysteriously disappeared and that in fact there was no "special account" in his name at all. This jolted him into taking an interest in his money, and trying to find out where it had gone and what his manager had done with it. Making Jimi financially dependent, so that he constantly had to go to his manager for money, was one of the tactics used to keep him under control.

money in his shoe, just in case he might need it.

Most people who came into contact with Jimi fell under the spell of his charm and genuine warmth, but even though he was usually surrounded by many people, he often felt lonely. He expressed this loneliness in some of his songs, such as "The Burning Of The Midnight Lamp" from 1967 and "My Friend" from 1968. In general, Jimi found it easier to relate to women. He felt that they understood him better than men, being more sympathetic to the sensitive and artistic side of his personality.

With all the success he had, you might assume that Jimi was confident in all things, but I found him to be quite an insecure person, always wanting to know your opinion, especially about his music.

His music was Jimi, and he cared deeply what those close to him thought about it. He could become artistically frustrated when his creativity wasn't flowing, but once new ideas came he was happy again.

"I know that people think I'm moody but that's only because I'm thinking of music most of the time. If I suddenly clam up it's because I've just hit on an idea." (Interview with Norrie Drummond, *New Musical Express*, June 1967)

Jimi couldn't stand it when people lied; this was one of the few things that really upset him. On one occasion in London in March 1968, he wanted to jam at the Speakeasy. He found a couple of musicians, including one he didn't know but who, like the New York cabbie, assured him he was a good player. Once they started playing, Jimi realized that the guy had no idea what he was doing. The problem was that Jimi was unable to stop the session straight away because the whole club was excited about hearing him play, and he didn't want to disappoint them. Afterwards Jimi was upset to find out from other musicians that the guy had lied to him, just so that he could later brag about once having jammed with Jimi Hendrix.

Some people have claimed that there were a couple of occasions when Jimi became violent. If this is true, then I believe that somebody must have provoked him. For violence was not in Jimi's nature – he did not like confrontation and tried to avoid it. I never saw him being violent or even coming close to it. I saw that when people really got on his nerves – and Jimi had a lot of patience – then he would just ignore them. Sometimes, when he was on tour and found that his equipment hadn't been set up properly, he would raise his voice in frustration. But a moment later he would apologize for doing so.

In the *Sounds* article quoted earlier, Bob Dawbarn also wrote: "Hendrix was warm, gentle and patient. I find it hard to equate the man who would leap to his feet to light your cigarette with the stories of smashed hotel rooms in Denmark. There must have been a dark side to his character. I can only say that I, personally, never saw the slightest sign of it."

After one concert in Göteborg, Sweden, in January 1968, Jimi had too much to drink, which seldom happened – alcohol didn't agree with him and he knew it. For several reasons, among them the fact that he was exhausted, he had become rather frustrated and nervous. In addition, he believed that someone had spiked his drink, which was fashionable in those days. When someone in the hotel began to annoy Jimi, he lost his usual self-control and reportedly smashed up his room, but without hurting anyone. The hotel staff called the police and Jimi was arrested.

However, that is just one side of the story. Jimi had worked constantly since he had been discovered in 1966, he and his band burdened with constant touring and recording. On top of this heavy schedule came an unpleasant court case with a small record company called PPX, over rights in some of Jimi's early recordings which had now come out under his name. On these recordings he had been principally a backing musician, so that now he was seriously upset and worried about his artistic reputation, fearing that his fans would think they were buying his present music.

Seriously stressed from overwork and the legal

I never saw him being violent or even coming close to it.

"Sometimes I'd like to tell the world off, but I just can't because it's not in my nature."

INTERVIEW WITH ALAN SMITH, HIT PARADE, NOVEMBER 1969

wrangles, Jimi desperately needed a break. He had asked many times for a holiday, but his wishes were ignored. The stress was enormous. One thing led to another, and it all ended in his lashing out in Sweden in the way he did.

Jimi had to stay in the police cell overnight. When he was asked the next morning what had happened, Jimi couldn't remember anything, but was very apologetic about the damage he had caused.

I would never deny that Jimi had his weaknesses. He was a highly evolved spirit, but as a person he was not infallible. He could be naive and impulsive, and sometimes would appear quite thoughtless, doing things without considering the consequences. Indeed in some respects he regarded himself as weak. Nevertheless, we should remember that at the time of his success he was still very young – and only twenty-seven when he died.

Bear in mind too that the sixties were a pretty wild time, notorious for searching and experimenting. Things were done spontaneously, without a second thought, and the keyword was freedom. Taking drugs was looked on as an important expression of this new-found liberation. A revolution, albeit in people's minds, was taking place: a rebellion against a rather narrow and oppressive establishment. The fifties were barely over, a decade when kids had to wear certain kinds of clothes and hairstyles, and were forced into all sorts of social conformity. "Breaking out" was a major preoccupation of the sixties: an attempt to live a life of experiences as far removed from society's norms as possible.

To some extent, Jimi took part in all this, being, but also playing, the restless rebel, and offering a new generation someone with whom they could identify. But he was a complex personality who was seen in a variety of ways. There were many facets to him both as a person and as an artist. But to gain a better understanding of Jimi, it is very important, I believe, to consider the great faith he had in God and the higher powers. He was not religious in the sense of subscribing to any particular conventional faith, but he was spiritual in a universal sense. Unfortunately for him, he met only a handful of people in his lifetime who recognized this side of him and who would listen and encourage him to speak about his inner faith, knowledge and feelings. This explains why for a long time he felt forced to keep this vital part of himself hidden.

JIMI FROM BEYOND

During our time together, some of my most significant experiences with Jimi were our discussions about his spiritual convictions. On many occasions when I was with him, he spoke on this subject in great detail, describing in the most vivid terms the spiritual world he had experienced. The core of his belief and his firm conviction was that there is more to our existence than just the visible and tangible parts: that there is life after death, and that there are many unseen links between the two worlds.

When I first met Jimi I had not previously come into contact with anyone holding such beliefs. Through our conversations he made me see things differently, and I slowly became aware that what he told me was somehow strangely familiar. It struck a chord in me; I felt a percussion within myself. But it was not just what he told me, but the way he put it all across: I found his certainty about his beliefs was overwhelming. He awakened me to something I had not been conscious of before; but I listened with amazement and fascination as a new world of wonders was opened to me, and my soul acknowledged it to be the truth. Jimi was also trying to convey the essence of this spiritual world through his music and lyrics.

Strangely enough, our talks were a new experience for Jimi, as it was the first time he had felt free to speak about his spiritual creed without reservations, outside any textual or musical context. He told me this himself several times, and he needed to reassure himself that I was really interested in what he was saying, because most people around him were not.

Jimi did not believe that we are born simply to die. He felt strongly that everything has a reason and a purpose, and that there would be no sense in life if there was nothing beyond death. He was certain that after death life continues in another world; that we leave our physical body behind and return to what we have always been: free spirits. Like a butterfly we slip out of our cocoon after our physical death, and return to the other side, the Spiritworld.

Jimi described parts of this world which he could remember, portraying it with passion and delight. He painted beautiful mystic scenes of green, lucid valleys, crystal rivers, waterfalls and mountain lakes; a world full of magic, where you could stand in amazement and discover places unseen and unheard of, passing mysterious golden cities

> "There's no telling how many lives your spirit will go through – die and be reborn."
>
> LIFE MAGAZINE, OCTOBER 1969

or encountering ancient temples materializing from nowhere. This was a land where the most beautiful sounds and sweet music could be heard, and the air was filled with a perfume more delicious than any fragrance on earth: a world of enchantment!

In a very special interview with Robin Richman for *Life* magazine in October 1969, Jimi for once cast aside restraint and spoke about this subject as frankly as possible, albeit on a philosophical level. In his own words: "The

If you don't want me this time around,

Yeah, I'll be glad to go back to Spiritland.

everyday mud world we're living in today compared to the spiritual world is like a parasite compared to the ocean and the ocean is the biggest living thing you know about. One way to approach the spiritual side is facing the truth....

"People want release from any kind of way nowadays. The idea is to release in the proper form. Then they'll feel like going into another world, a clearer world. The music flows from the air; that's why I can connect with a spirit, and when they come down off this natural high, they see clearer, feel different things – don't think of pain and hurting the next person.

"There's no telling how many lives your spirit will go through – die and be reborn. Like my mind will be back in the days when I was a flying horse. Before I can remember anything, I can remember music and stars and planets. I could go to sleep and write fifteen symphonies. I had very strange feelings that I was here [on earth] for something and I was going to get a chance to be heard."

Jimi also talked about life in the Spiritworld, which is characterized by harmony and peace, rather than conflict and competition. There is no need for aggressive behaviour in a world where everyone recognizes one another as a brother or sister, and appreciates differences and different levels of evolution, not as a source of conflict, but as something completely self-evident and natural.

Moreover, in the Spiritworld everyone is aware of the meaning and value of his or her life – unlike on earth, where so many people do not understand their true identity or what they want to achieve in life, let alone what the meaning of it could be. Many strive for a lifetime to find an answer which is within themselves all along.

Once we return to the Spiritworld we regain the full individual and universal knowledge that each of us has gathered since the day our spirit was born. Some of us – as a spirit – have lived for thousands of years.

While we are here on earth we go through a period of learning, suffering and, hopefully, evolving – as if in a school – while in the Spiritworld we go through a period of putting our old and new knowledge into action.

Most people confine the horizon of their consciousness to the material world. Jimi, being at home on "both sides of the sky", as he put it, tried to persuade people to broaden their horizon in order to become full human and spiritual beings. He wanted them to appreciate the entirety of our creation, comprising both the earth we know and the Spiritworld we come from. For both are intertwined and essential to each other, and this knowledge can help us to achieve further spiritual evolution.

As Jimi explained all this to me I became aware that he was also inhabiting this "other" world – in his thoughts, his dreams, and in his work. I came to understand that this dimension was the source of his tremendous faith, giving him the strength he needed. It made him look at life in a different, more objective way than most of the people around him.

The influence of this other world can clearly be felt in his music and his lyrics. In one of his songs, "Voodoo Child (slight return)", he says:

If I don't meet you no more in this world,
I'll meet you on the next one, so don't be late.

In another song, "Belly Button Window", he, as a foetus in the womb, sings:

If you don't want me this time around,
Yeah, I'll be glad to go back to Spiritland.

To fully appreciate Jimi Hendrix and his work, it is vital to understand that this hidden realm was the genuine source of his inspiration and the driving force enabling him to continue the destiny he had to pursue. Without the strength he derived from this power-giving and elevating element, he would never have been able to survive for as long as he did the attacks and obstacles of profit-seeking businessmen and some thoughtless people who surrounded him.

This whole concept of spirituality is vitally important in order to do justice to and to fully understand Jimi Hendrix. It makes no difference what one thinks or believes personally: as far as Jimi was concerned, the spiritual side of things was not just a game, but a serious reality. Anyone who has a genuine interest in Jimi and his work should not fail to take this aspect of him into account.

I can only say how utterly convincing Jimi was on this subject, and how firm in his belief. I still share his belief and I feel that, although Jimi may be physically dead, he is still active and alive in another world. He has simply left his earth-body behind, and is maybe watching us with amusement – as Jimi from beyond.

If I don't meet you no more in this world,

I'll meet you on the next one, so don't be late.

BREAKING

In this portrait Jimi is gazing at the onlooker – trying to communicate something he felt was important for everyone to realize and understand; something which was very close to his heart: breaking the chains of illusion.

Jimi told me of his conviction that in this world people keep absorbing worthless information, blocking the paths to their inner knowledge and keeping their senses from being in tune with their own truth and the laws of God. He believed that so many people were being lost because they had been programmed with the wrong information from the time they were born.

When a baby is born, Jimi maintained, its mind is clear and untouched, like a rock-crystal, until people start to influence and programme its ways of thinking in order to fit it into the established system. The biggest problem is that the "teachers" themselves often do not know enough, because they are given teaching programmes and have neither the will nor the insight to separate useful information from all the rubbish they feed us. Jimi believed in particular that we should forget about the past, or at least the irrelevant elements of the past, in order to be able to embark on a completely new way of thinking.

"If people would stop blaming, you can see how frustrating it is, you take the black person who argues with the white person that he's been badly treated for the last two hundred years, but now's the time to work it out instead of talking about the past. We know the past is all screwed up, and so instead of talking about the past, they should get it all together again. Then the white man will argue something else, but that's all little child games. Arguments...that's for kids, you know where the truth is. The truth is that it's time to get together now." (Interview with Jacoba Atlas, *TeenSet*, January 1969)

All useless information should be left behind, as well as the hypocritical rules which tell people what to do in order to be materially successful. Children are being brainwashed and moulded in accordance with such illusions, being made slaves of the system, with all its misguided and misleading values: values that are destroying our intuitive powers, the very source of the beautiful ideas and thoughts of which we are capable.

Jimi criticized the commercials on television and the effect they have on people's minds. "Maybe we can just scare half the people with common sense. Take cancer and cigarettes on TV – we don't say yes and we don't say no, we just tell the truth. You blind your head to the TV all of the time by watching some dreary program – really the fantasy side of life! – and then you say, 'I'll just get a joint and do this.' But the problem is still there. When you come back out, it's there, the street is there." (Interview with Jacoba Atlas, *Circus*, March 1969)

People should take some time for themselves

> "We know the past is all screwed up, and so instead of talking about the past, they should get it all together again."

instead, to think and check out what is really happening. Instead they are ultimately full of information which doesn't come from within, but only from outside sources. If they would just take the time to concentrate on themselves and what is happening around them, they would soon see that in reality they know nothing about themselves, as they never had a chance to study and discover their inner self.

Jimi also believed that it is so easy to take another road: if you are serious, all it takes is a few minutes each day. I can still hear him saying that a lot of time in this world is wasted on all sorts of unimportant things, but when it comes down to something as essential as inner development and understanding of the world, people just can't be bothered. This is the reason why Jimi was trying to help people find the path again, through his messages and his music. He wanted them to

discover their true self, their spiritual dimension, in order to become aware of themselves, of this world, and the true laws of life.

He especially criticized modern society for allowing money and materialism to rule, not giving a chance to anything else. In Jimi's view, those people who are continually trying to gain more worldly wealth are masters of nothing but error and illusion. For such ephemeral things will not last, but melt into the sea, like "Castles Made Of Sand".

Jimi also expressed to me his conviction that, because people are running after the wrong things – money, jobs, prestige etc. – they are frustrated and depressed. No money can buy the truly important things in life, like love, friendship, harmony, peace, trust, understanding and faith. Money can only supply us with the material and visible, but is powerless where real and everlasting values are concerned. Such values are nevertheless necessary if

No money can buy the truly

friendship, harmony, peace,

one is to live and grow spiritually.

However, Jimi felt that people could improve their situation by taking an honest viewpoint and living more in terms of feeling and intuition. What really matters in the end is not our name, our social position, or how much money we've got in the bank: all these "achievements" amount to nothing in the eyes of the Lord. It is the development of our soul and what we make of our lives that really count. The soul must rule the ways of life – not money, cars or drugs.

So it is us, Jimi believed, who can change the world: by opening our eyes and taking a good look at what is going on around us. Each of us, he felt, has a responsibility, not just to ourselves, but for the state the world is in. If in my painting Jimi is looking straight at the observer, it is because he is urging all of us to help change this world into the place it is meant to be.

important things in life, like love,

rust, understanding and faith.

"I'm daydreaming!"

RAINY DAY – DREAM AWAY

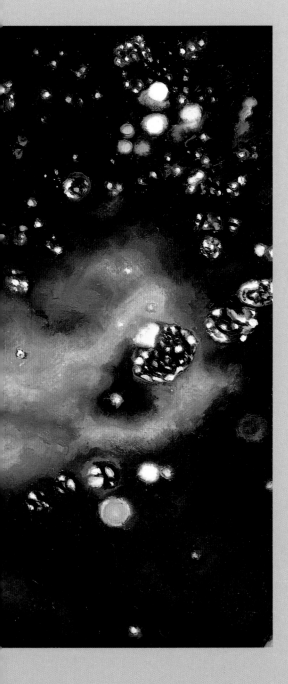

Sometimes when I telephoned Jimi while he was abroad, and asked him what he was doing, he would reply, "I'm daydreaming!" This for him was another way of saying that he was waiting to be inspired, or was already being inspired, at times listening to music, at other times visualizing pictures and visions and also hearing music in his head. In this painting I tried to capture Jimi "daydreaming".

Noel and Mitch, his bass player and drummer, sometimes jokingly called Jimi "The Bat", because he would go into his hotel room, draw all the curtains and put his coloured scarves all over the lampshades. Then he would play his guitar, or just lie on the bed and daydream. He told me that by doing so he was creating an atmosphere which helped him to be inspired, to create a new song or to get new ideas, cutting himself off from the outside world, creating his own world inside. He explained that this was a form of meditation.

Later on I found out that his recording engineer, Eddie Kramer, used a similar method to get Jimi into a mood in which it was easier for him to lose himself in his music, especially when it came to recording vocals. Eddie would dim the lights in the studio and create an atmosphere that made Jimi feel more at ease.

Jimi told me that he also sometimes meditated in a more conventional way by sitting down, letting his mind wander, and allowing complete peace of mind to emerge within himself. He wanted me to start meditating as well, but warned me to be patient and not to expect immediate results. He knew people who had tried it but had given up after a while because nothing was happening, which may occur if you expect substantial results in too short a time. He pointed out that some people could have an instant "opening" and receive visions straight away. With others it might take a little longer to get results, perhaps six months or more.

Jimi was not in favour of any form of pressure or rigid meditative discipline. He let his feelings be his guide and would only meditate when he felt like it. However, having practised it for a long time, he had developed something like an invisible switch, letting inspiration come through really fast. He told me that it was important to get into a certain condition to let the inspiration flow, and that it was vital for your creativity to keep stress and worries out, not to let them block your flow of energy. If this state is achieved, meditation can be a great tool for gaining inner peace. Through his own experience, Jimi let me know that meditation can help you to discover a great deal about yourself and the worlds within and around you.

He also told me that it helps to have a candle burning, to serve as a sign to your friends in Spiritland that you want their guidance.

LISTENING TO THE SOUNDS OF THE UNIVERSE

Here Jimi is listening to the universe, receiving music from the spheres; suns and galaxies are swirling around his mind.

The galaxy resembles the human brain or the first division of an egg cell, which symbolizes birth and fresh creativity – the birth of a new life, an idea or a project being generated from a creative nucleus. All is contained in that cell, waiting to be developed and to materialize.

The united colours of primary red and orange are the first colours of the spectrum we are able to see. These are the colours of dawn.

The painting depicts the moment when Jimi has a sudden inspiration. His attention is absorbed, taking it all in, receiving. The suns resemble atoms, sparks of ideas, with the galaxy as the source of something about to be born.

The new beginning was an important concept for Jimi. He called a new album which he intended to release in 1969 *First Rays Of The New Rising Sun*. It was typical of him to make a fresh start in music, as well as in life, when something no longer felt right. Things had to be right for him to be able to be creative. This way of thinking is also expressed by the last two sentences of Jimi's poem on the inside cover of the *Band Of Gypsys* album:

Afterwards baby child sipped a heartful of ocean. Spat out the waste and walked upon the NEW DAY.

LEGENDS

Jimi shared with me a feeling of closeness to the Native Americans – the North American Indians. He was also a member of that race, and this gave me the idea for this painting, which I completed and Jimi saw in 1969.

For the Indians, the carved wooden totem pole relates the entire family legend in the form of a pictograph. Only an understanding of what the symbols mean to the Indians allows the totem pole to be interpreted. Each figure represents an important symbolic constituent of a story or myth relating to a particular tribe.

Jimi told me that for certain periods in his childhood he had lived with his grandmother, Nora, whose own grandmother had been a full-blooded Cherokee princess. He was fascinated when she told him stories and legends of her ancestors. She had even made some original Indian clothes for Jimi, although when he wore them to school the other children made fun of him.

Nevertheless Jimi listened eagerly when his grandmother talked about the way the Indians lived, and their spiritual beliefs, rituals and magic. She described a world that seemed to him at the same time both far away and familiar: a world in which everyone was trying to live in harmony with the Creator and his Creation. These "primitive" people, he understood, had found a way of living in accord with themselves and their natural environment – by feeling themselves to be part of the planet earth and nature. At the same time they had developed an evolved religion and philosophy, combining the powers of nature and spirit. They were, according to Jimi, people who truly understood "both sides of the sky".

Cherokee mythology traditionally said that their tribe had come from the skies. In their religion and cosmology, they preserved legends and myths in which everything down to the smallest insect had its specific meaning and position. They believed that each stone, each plant, each tree – everything in nature – was filled with vital power and had its own purpose and significance. Jimi felt close to these ideas, and in talking about them he also revealed to me details of his own philosophy of nature and its powers.

The Cherokees had an original culture with its own language. They knew how to read and write, had schools and libraries, and had built up a sophisticated social system. Jimi expressed to me his conviction that the Indians were not the primitive people which the white man had portrayed through the ages, but on the contrary were a deeply spiritual and evolved race.

For a long time the Cherokees had developed and lived in a society of peace and harmony, and they had tried to create and sustain peaceful relations with the white men who had invaded their land. However, their efforts did not protect them from slaughter and imprisonment, for the white people were interested not in peace but in territorial gain. In the end the Cherokee society collapsed and the nation was destroyed.

Jimi told me that the song "I Don't Live Today" dealt with the desperate struggle of the North American Indians.

He expresses clearly the pain the North American tribes must have undergone in losing their freedom and identity. No longer free to roam the endless plains of North America, they were confined to camps like prisoners, forced to lead a life completely unnatural to them. They were not living – merely existing.

And still today, apart from some minor improvements, these true natives of the North American continent are forced to live subject to the laws of their usurpers, still experiencing discrimination and suffering, often just wasting their time through being deprived of their native ways and social structures.

So, spiritually, Jimi felt closest to the North American Indian race, which he demonstrated by frequently wearing headbands and beautifully crafted Indian silver and turquoise jewellery. Indeed he believed he had been an American Indian in a past life. I remember him giving me details of what he could recall. In that previous life he had been Wasami, meaning Thunder, and this was the name he wanted to give our possible future son.

Jimi believed he had been an American Indian in a past life.

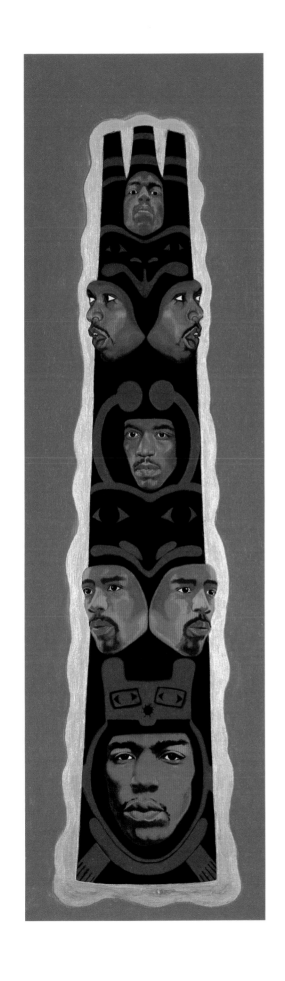

Will I live tomorrow,

Well I just can't say,

Will I live tomorrow,

Well I just can't say,

But I know for sure

I don't live today

No sun coming through

my windows,

Feel like I'm living at

the bottom of a grave...

IN FROM THE STORM

Jimi loved the city of New York, that vibrant and exciting place with its own electric force.

In this painting he is standing in the middle of New York, surrounded by thunder and lightning, like a lightning-conductor between the higher dimensions and the earth.

Jimi had first arrived in New York in 1964, after leaving the army and touring for three years through various American states with many different artists, including Little Richard, Chuck Jackson, Jackie Wilson, B.B. King, Otis Redding, the Isley Brothers and Ike and Tina Turner.

Although still an unknown backing musician, he came to New York with high hopes, confident that he would make it. Yet this was one of the toughest parts of his career. As he told me later, he sometimes did not have enough money to buy food and at times had to sleep on the streets. On the other hand, more than once people helped him out, especially women who saw him struggling and offered him a place to stay. He never forgot the generous help he received in those times of need. In a taped interview with Meatball Fulton in December 1967, Jimi confirmed, "I used to be on the block, starving, you know. And girls used to help me out and all that, you know. Girls are some of my best friends because they used to help me. Really help me."

Jimi also told me that this period was an important experience for him.

It was also in New York, in July 1966, that Chas Chandler, his future manager, discovered Jimi while he was playing with his own group, Jimmy James and the Blue Flames, at the Cafe Wha?. Chandler persuaded Jimi to go to Britain and try to build a career there.

After he had become successful in England, he returned to New York for the first time in June 1967. That same month he played in California at the Monterey International Pop Festival – the breakthrough concert appearance which made Jimi famous in America. Between his extensive tours, he settled down in New York and made it his home.

Jimi was convinced that all races were equal, and that all differences between individuals were meant to be and had their own distinct meanings. He therefore loved the melting-pot of New York, where people of all colours, races and cultures met and lived together. Jimi enjoyed diving into the excitement and the vibrations of this city – sharing the nearly limitless creativity of so many artists and musicians in the late sixties. This creativity was the expression of a cultural movement which Jimi put his stamp on to a considerable extent.

New York in those days seemed to be the centre of an exciting world, a world where it all happened, and it was natural for Jimi to make it his creative home. He especially enjoyed the possibility of jamming any day of the week with musicians from all musical directions – blues, rock and roll, rhythm and blues, or jazz.

A dream of Jimi's was to have his own studio, giving him the opportunity to play and record whenever he felt creative and inspired. He loved spending nights and days experimenting with different sounds and musical ideas, and couldn't wait for his dream to come true. He soon made plans with his then manager, Mike Jeffery, to build such a studio in New York.

However, in 1969 Jimi was forced to take Jeffery in on the project on a fifty-fifty basis, as he had been advised that he didn't have the financial potential to finance and build the studio on his own. Jimi disliked the idea from the start, but even more so when he later heard from other people that Jeffery was borrowing some of the money to build the studio from the Mafia. However, there was nothing Jimi could do about it at that time, and it was at this point that he began to feel uncomfortable in New York, and to make plans to stop his association with Jeffery as his manager.

"I used to be on the block, starving, you know. And girls used to help me out... Really help me."

THE CONSCIENCE OF AMERICA

This painting shows Jimi playing guitar in front of a huge ocean wave. In the distance the Statue of Liberty is about to be engulfed by the water, her robe soiled and bloodstained and her flame extinguished.

Inspired by a line in one of Jimi's lyrics, "and then New York drowns as we held hands", the painting shows two conflicting sides of the United States of America. The Statue of Liberty is the effigy of America's soul. It symbolizes the spirit embodied in the nation's written Constitution. But the America in which Jimi grew up was far from adhering to those high ideals. The nation's conscience had been defiled so much by corruption and bloodshed that only a radical new beginning could change what had been wrong for so long, and bring new hope.

This is one of the central themes of Jimi's message: the need for complete renewal and a radically different approach. Jimi felt that narrow-mindedness and petty thinking, in conjunction with greed and hypocrisy, were among the main reasons why these ideals were never fully realized. It was part of his mission to point a powerful finger at those double standards.

This is exactly what he did in full view of the whole world, by playing "The Star Spangled Banner" at Woodstock in the summer of 1969, in a way that this music had never been expressed before. Transforming his guitar into a war machine of sound, he tore through the sanctimonious veil of political double-dealing at the height of the Vietnam war, and turned his nation's anthem into a representation of a battleground.

In an interview with Sue Clark in December 1969, Jimi said, "It's time for a new national anthem. America is divided into two definite divisions... Something has to happen or else you can just keep on dragging along with the program, which is based upon the past and is always dusty."

Jimi became a voice of the conscience of America. Through powerful artistic statements, directed against the war in Vietnam, Jimi drew attention to what was wrong in society at that time. He helped the nation to wake up and begin to redefine its view of right and wrong, of lost and found. He was not afraid of showing the ugly side of America or of pointing the alternative way forward. Having grown up there in the forties and fifties, and being of mixed race, Jimi had plenty of first-hand experience of, and insight into, how the textbook values of freedom and equality for all were being misinterpreted by society.

The ocean wave in the painting symbolizes the spiritual emotion Jimi encapsulated – the wave of conscience. He was at the very crest of a huge wave of renewal, of realization and of maturation. His music and lyrics genuinely helped to change the awareness and attitudes of many people in America and all over the world.

In 1969 and 1970, within Jimi's close environs in New York, he was confronted by some ugly realities. He was bursting with ideas, but for more than a year before his death his artistic output was to be sabotaged by other people. He was also to go through a lot of other changes.

Jimi wanted to develop, expand, and move on in many fields. In 1969 he intended to change and develop his music, but unfortunately faced strong opposition from his manager, who tried to make Jimi repeat the style of music which initially had made him famous: for example, "Hey Joe" and "Purple Haze". Mike Jeffery tried to persuade Jimi to stay in line and do what he was told to do. Persuasion meant any means necessary, including strong threats.

Jeffery was not a guy to mess around with. He said that he had been a British secret agent in MI6 and kept circulating stories of having done undercover work, including killing people. A specialist in all sorts of things, he knew all the tricks of the trade and early on in his career had had connections with the Newcastle crime scene. Now he had got involved with the New York Mafia, and was also into the occult. He developed close links with one person in particular who had connections with a brutal dictatorship, mercenaries and the Mafia.

He was at the very crest of a huge wave of renewal, of realization and of maturation.

Jimi felt more and more unsafe in New York, the city where he used to feel so much at home. It had begun to seem like a prison to him, and a place where he had to watch his back all the time.

In May 1969 Jimi was arrested at Toronto Airport for possession of drugs. He later told me he believed Jeffery had used a third person to plant the drugs on him – as a warning and to teach him a lesson.

Jeffery had realized not only that Jimi was looking for ways of breaking out of their contract, but also that Jimi was searching for his missing money, which Jeffery was hiding somewhere. Jeffery might have calculated that the Toronto arrest would be an easy way to silence Jimi. There were enough recordings on tape for at least three, maybe four, albums. Or maybe if no witness came forward in Jimi's defence, Jeffery might have already planned to provide a "witness". The whole Toronto affair really upset Jimi and it took him weeks to get back into his creative flow.

His New York dreams had dissolved like "Castles Made Of Sand".

At the same time Jimi was looking for new musicians to work and play with. His dream was to find good players who would also be his friends, which was the reason he chose Billy Cox as a new bass player when Noel Redding left the band. Jimi and Billy had met many years earlier, in the army. Percussionist Jerry Velez and multi-instrumentalist Juma Sultan would also join Jimi's new group, playing the Woodstock Festival in August 1969, among other gigs.

Jeffery did not like Jimi to have friends who would put ideas in his head and give him strength. He preferred Jimi to be more isolated, or to mix with certain people whom Jeffery could use to influence and try to manipulate him.

So in New York Jimi felt at times that he was under surveillance, and others around him noticed the same. He tried desperately to get out of his management contract, and asked several people for advice on the best way to do it.

Jimi started to notice which people around him could no longer be trusted, as things he had told them in confidence now filtered through to Jeffery.

Obviously some people informed his manager of Jimi's plans, possibly having been bought or promised advantages by Jeffery. Jimi had always been a trusting and open person, but now he had reason to become suspicious of people he didn't know well, becoming quite secretive and keeping very much to himself. Juma Sultan informed Jimi that Jeffery had even tried to buy him off, in order to keep him away from Jimi.

While Jimi was in a house near Woodstock, practising for the Festival, Jeffery and some Italian Mafia types dropped by and told him that he had to play at the opening night of the Salvation, a New York club with strong Mafia connections. Jimi had refused before, but while Jeffery went into the house to persuade Jimi to do the gig, the other men stayed outside and started some target practice with a gun. Jimi understood the message and did the gig.

There were several more incidents intended to intimidate Jimi, and his band were also threatened that they should play certain clubs – or else. However, the most menacing incident took place in the autumn of 1969, when Jimi was visited by two men. They said they had been sent by Jeffery to pick up Jimi, and he believed them. The next thing Jimi knew, he had been kidnapped, and the men told him they belonged to the Mafia.

Jimi was hidden in a warehouse somewhere in New York. At first Jimi believed that they would kill him, but as time passed and nothing happened he realized something else was going on. While he was a prisoner they threatened him, but did not hurt him, so Jimi could not figure out what they wanted. The next day he was told to call Jeffery and

let him know that Jimi was dead unless the manager handed over the contract he had with Jimi. Then, all of a sudden, and seemingly out of nowhere, Jeffery's people turned up and "rescued" Jimi.

When he had recovered from the shock, Jimi came to the conclusion that Jeffery, unbeknown to the people who rescued him, had been behind the kidnapping from the start, and that the whole thing had been staged to bring Jimi into line and make him realize just how much he was in Jeffery's power. The simple message seemed to be that if Jeffery wanted, he could do anything to Jimi.

But this didn't stop Jimi trying even harder to get out of his contract with Jeffery. The biggest problem was that if Jimi just walked out of the contract, Jeffery would still keep the rights to a considerable amount of unpublished material. Jimi feared that if he lost control of this Jeffery would be able to manipulate the tapes according to his own commercial taste, by having the music and message changed, rearranged and effectively destroyed.

This was the main reason for Jimi's staying with his manager for so long. It was simply a blackmail situation. Jimi was desperately trying to find a way to cancel his management arrangements while retaining control of the music he had been recording in the meantime.

While all this was going on, other pressures continued. In June 1969 Jimi's old group, with Mitch Mitchell and Noel Redding, had broken up. At the Woodstock Festival in August Jimi played with Billy Cox as well as Juma Sultan, guitarist Larry Lee, Jerry Velez and Mitch Mitchell. He called this new group Gypsy Sun and Rainbows. After Woodstock this formation disbanded and Jimi put together a new group, returning to the three-piece concept. It was called the Band Of

Gypsys, and Billy Cox played the bass and Buddy Miles the drums.

In the meantime a legal settlement had given the rights for one future Jimi Hendrix album to Ed Chalpin, a manager who had put Jimi under contract back in 1965. The *Band Of Gypsys* album was culled from two of four concert appearances on 31 December 1969 and 1 January 1970. The band was under-rehearsed, and Jimi was very dissatisfied with the results of the concerts, which were nevertheless released as his next album. Again Jimi had had no chance to participate in a business decision that was of great importance to him on an artistic level. After a fifth and final concert, later in January, the Band Of Gypsys fell apart.

Business deals and financial power-play gave Jeffery a legal stranglehold on Jimi as well. The Jimi Hendrix Experience was Jeffery's main source of income and he was determined to squeeze as much as he could out of this successful formula. In 1970 problems and pressures on Jimi accumulated, as several lawsuits were tying up his money and he was in debt as a result of the building of a recording studio in New York.

In the meantime Jeffery tried to push Jimi into reforming the Experience, but with no success. Through the last months of 1969 and the beginning of 1970, Jimi tried to bring out some new material, but was stopped by his management, who thought the songs to be too spiritual and not commercial enough. In between, he kept on trying to find the missing money and a way out of his management contract. As Jeffery would tell me later, at a meeting after Jimi's death, Jimi had made seven attempts in all to free himself.

There were now only a few people Jimi could still trust in New York. He had become more and more isolated, which suited the intentions of his

manager very well. He faced all kinds of demands, and often, just to get away from them, he would leave his Greenwich Village flat and hide at a friend's place. This sometimes went on for days because of the heavy pressure from his manager and other people and organizations who wanted to use Jimi for their own purposes, at the same time making it hard for him to be creative.

In May 1970 Jimi started his "Cry of Love" tour, which took him all over America and lasted until August. In the meantime his recording studio in New York, the Electric Lady Studio, had been completed, and he started recording there. Although the studio had been built for his purposes, Jimi was not the sole owner, for Jeffery had managed to obtain a fifty per cent share. On 26 August a party was held to mark the official opening of the studio. Many people attended, but Jimi took part reluctantly, and left early, because he felt it was not his studio any more. People were involved who were not acting on his behalf. But the worst thing was that he did not have the money to buy out his manager's share.

So when Jimi left America for the last time that same day, his New York dreams had dissolved like "Castles Made Of Sand". Of New York he had said the previous year: "I mean as a physical city it's doomed completely, demoralized like Pompeii. It's nothing bad though. It's just what happens when people get lost." (Interview with Jacoba Atlas, *TeenSet*, January 1969)

On 27 August Jimi arrived in London. He explained to me at that time that New York was artistically as exciting and stimulating as ever, but for him, life there had just become impossible, and he had to get away from it. In one of the interviews he gave in London he said: "New York's killing me at the moment. It's positively claustrophobic! Things go so fast, you might as well get ready to step on a roller-coaster every time you move outside your door... There's no place like London!" (Interview with Mike Ledgerwood, *Disc and Music Echo*, September 1970) It was like a confession – declaring one place his home, while turning his back on another.

"There is all this violent thing in the States right now. It's really a clash between the new and the old. They make black and white fight against each other so they can take over at each end."

INTERVIEW WITH BOB DAWBARN, *MELODY MAKER*, 8 MARCH 1969

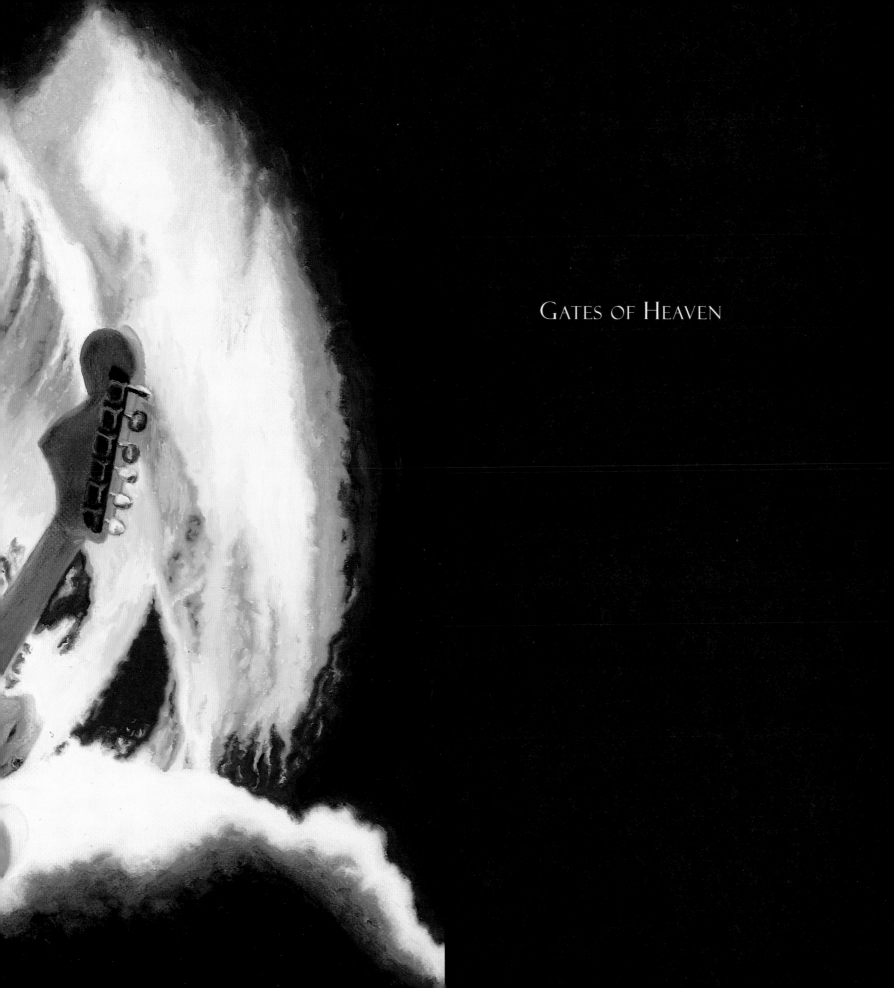

GATES OF HEAVEN

WATERFALL

This painting was inspired by listening to Jimi's "May This Be Love", from his first album, *Are You Experienced*. Jimi told me that the original title of the song was "Waterfall", but that it was then changed into "May This Be Love".

When I asked Jimi about the meaning of this song and its lyric, he explained that he was talking about the ever-flowing stream of inspiration, represented by the image of a waterfall. Water is a very powerful spiritual force. The waterfall represents life, movement, constant change. Jimi said it generates powers, and as long as his river of inspiration flowed he would have no worries.

Jimi told me that the words "my rainbow calling me" refer to his destiny and task on earth to convey his own special messages.

He felt that there were three main sources from which his knowledge came. One is recollection of the inner knowledge, which can only be remembered by awakening one's own spirit through thinking, meditation and suffering. The second source of knowledge is remembering astral experiences. The third is inspiration by other spirits.

I wanted to know whether by that he meant something like guardian angels. Jimi nodded his head, saying that it might seem strange to some people, but he felt comfort and even joy when he sensed their presence, and it made him happy when he knew they were around. The song "Angel", for example, recorded in 1970, reflects this sense.

Jimi was convinced that the spirits around him were benevolent and wanted to help him. Without their inspiration, he believed, he would not have been able to achieve the music he created.

In the title song of *Are You Experienced*, he told me, he had been talking about the inspiration he kept receiving from beyond:

Trumpets and violins
I can hear in the distance.
I think they're calling our names
Maybe now
You can't hear them
But you will
If you just take hold of my hand.

Jimi explained that the distant trumpets and violins symbolize the message and the music he could hear from the other world. Trumpets stand for prophecies, while violins represent music. By becoming inspired, he said, he could pick up that music and those messages from the spirit dimension, and somehow translate them into his own musical and lyrical forms. (The trumpet, he explained, heralds something new appearing on the horizon.)

He said there was no need to be afraid of spirits, as long as they are positive ones, and was sure that all people on earth get inspired – some more than others – by their brothers and sisters from the other world. We are all inspired, but it is such a natural thing that most people don't listen, and are not receptive. Artists and women experience more such inspiration than others because in general they are more sensitive.

Jimi went on to state that certain people on earth, for example politicians, become used as "instruments" in order to achieve positive effects for the world. On the other hand, there are also evil spirits, but Jimi wanted to talk about that some other time.

He pointed out that certain spirits, guardian angels, were guiding people here on earth. They watch over us, and in dangerous situations can send us important ideas, or can even rescue us. He explained that only very few spirits are angels in the

Waterfall
Nothing can harm me at all
My worries seem so very small
With my waterfall

I can see my rainbow calling me
Through the misty breeze of my waterfall.

true sense of the word. When I asked him whether everyone had a spirit guide, he was confident that every person on earth has at least one spirit guide who looks after him or her if not rejected, but that there could be two or more. He said they could well be brothers or sisters from your own spirit dimension, from where you originally came; or they could be a deceased relative or a loved one with whom there existed a strong bond while this person was still on earth.

Astral Travel

In this painting I have tried to represent a spirit in the form of an eagle leaving earth, travelling at night into another dimension – the astral plane.

Jimi was fascinated by the spiritual side of everything and the purpose and meaning of life. He was an explorer, not only into music but also other areas of life, especially those connected with spirituality.

One day he asked me if I knew anything about astral travel. I told him that I didn't have a clue. He explained that while a person is living on earth his or her spirit could actually leave the body for a period of time. In fact he was sure that many people experienced astral travel without becoming consciously aware of it. Normally, he said, the spirit only hovers above the body for a certain time to recharge itself with cosmic energy – for the spirit is of an extremely fine texture, a form of energy.

Jimi also explained that a spirit may quite often leave the body at night. The more evolved and spiritually active a person is, the more easily will his spirit be able to travel to Spiritland, and meet the spirits of the dead. These are real astral journeys, and Jimi told me that they can be beautiful beyond description. The colours in Spiritland are much more intense than those on earth. They shine from within, and they seem to be almost living. At the same time there are sounds to be heard which are out of this world in the true sense of the words. Jimi would later try to reproduce some of these sounds in the studio, explaining to Eddie Kramer, his sound engineer, "I have heard these sounds in my dreams!"

Jimi told me about some of his astral journeys to mystical and magical dimensions, and I was fascinated. Some of his songs, he explained, were also triggered by astral travels which he had experienced in the past and was able to remember. He pointed out to me that often when he was asked how he got the idea for a certain song, he would answer, "I had a dream."

When I asked Jimi whether he had ever mentioned to journalists or anyone else that some of his songs were about astral travel, he explained that, apart from me, only a few people knew about it. But then, with a smile on his face, he said that soon more people would know, as he had written, among others, a song called "Astro Man". He told me that in this song he talked about himself going off on astral travel.

Jimi tried to describe to me what an incredible experience it was to go on the astral plane and how overwhelmed he was by the magic he encountered there. He believed that you can gain a lot of knowledge if you manage to recall those journeys. Most people, however, forget them or maybe think they were just dreams.

He also explained the difference between dreams and astral travel. You would remember an astral journey as an extraordinarily vivid dream. The

"Astro Man now he's flying across the stars."

Just wrap me up
in your wings, hear
what I said carry me o
Take me through your
dreams - Inside your
world, I want to be —
until tommorrow no
tears will you shed —
hold on till the
sun get out of bed

events in such a "dream" would feel as real and tangible as things experienced on earth. He encouraged me to try to remember my astral travel. Later on, while we were still talking about the same subject, he asked me if I had ever noticed that when I went to sleep with a major problem on my mind, the next morning I would wake up with the solution in my head. He believed that while we are on the astral plane we can be given solutions to our problems or answers to our questions.

He added that people who are not spiritually active, but identify with materialistic pursuits, have greater difficulty letting themselves go and only rarely experience astral travel.

Jimi also believed that when you are separated from a person here on earth you can nevertheless be together during the night, meeting for a certain period of time on the astral plane. When I asked him if he had written any songs on this theme, he said a few, two examples being "Spanish Castle Magic" and "Night Bird Flying":

She's just a night bird flying through
the night flying on home
She's just a night bird making a
midnight flight, sail on, sail on
Well, she's flying down to me
But till tomorrow gotta set her free,
set her free.

Another of these songs, Jimi told me, was "Izabella", at the beginning of which he says, "Hey, Izabella, girl, I am holding you in my dreams every night."

"Voodoo Chile" is another example:

Well I make love to you
And Lord knows you'll feel no pain.
Say I make love to you in your
sleep
And Lord knows you felt no pain.
'Cause I'm a million miles away and
at the same time
I am right here in your picture
frame,
'Cause I'm a Voodoo Chile,
Lord knows, I'm a Voodoo Chile.

I must say that at first all this seemed downright incredible to me. Jimi was the first person to tell me about the spiritual side of life and beyond. I noticed that after I had listened to this information, his songs gained more depth and meaning than I had ever realized before. From then on, I asked him, whenever time permitted, to explain to me in depth his lyrics and the message he was trying to convey. Often I wrote down his explanations and the stories behind his lyrics, especially after he came up with the idea of my doing an oil painting for each of his songs so that everyone would understand his message better.

Jimi's sincerity and deep belief in what he was saying inevitably convinced me that what I considered impossible was possible after all.

THE POET

I remember well that Jimi sometimes, all of a sudden, in the middle of a conversation, would become silent and seem miles away. He would then quickly grab any piece of paper he could lay hands on – a sheet of scrap paper, a matchbox or, if we were in a restaurant, a paper napkin – and write something down.

People who knew and understood him were familiar with this behaviour, knowing that ideas could come to him wherever he was. Some of his lyrics were written on an aeroplane while he was flying from one gig to another. However, to someone who didn't understand the way his mind worked, it must have looked peculiar, which made some people give Jimi a reputation for being "spaced out" and disorganized. In fact, he was very organized about things that were important to him. On the other hand, it is true that he could be quite negligent of things he had no interest in. For instance, as money meant nothing to him, he just didn't care about organizing it, taking the risk of his business being run down through the mishandling of his affairs by his manager, Mike Jeffery.

However, I learned that this was never as thoughtless as it may have appeared. To achieve great results as an artist, it is probably indispensable to allow oneself to flow with artistic energy, which is exactly what Jimi was doing, at least most of the time. Obviously this means that one always runs the risk of becoming controlled by circumstances, but it was a price that Jimi accepted. So, characteristically, the "chaotic" part of his career was almost entirely on the business side, never the artistic.

What amazed me most was when I saw him write down a complete lyric in hardly any time, without much reflection, just as if he were writing a letter. It seemed as if the whole lyric was flowing right through him, and he was trying to put it down on paper as quickly as he could.

But his lyrics did not always come to him that easily. Occasionally he would have more of a struggle to get something down. This usually happened when he had composed a song and then intended to fit a lyric to the music – which is naturally harder than writing the words without having the music prepared.

Without a doubt, Jimi was an exceptionally inspired writer. The artistic strength of his words, as well as his sense for the unexpected, original phrase, make it a delight to listen to his lyrics, especially when combined with music that in most cases provides a perfect balance to the words. He sometimes emphasized certain important parts of the lyrics by musical means, and to read his words simply as poems would therefore be to neglect the significance of this unity.

When playing live or in the studio, Jimi often used to improvise his lyrics – sometimes just a word or two, sometimes more drastically. It was the same with his music, which he never delivered in the same way twice, always breathing new life into it. For Jimi, his lyrics often had a very personal meaning. The same went for certain expressions, names and symbols. Many of these were derived from visions, a sphere of experience which for most people on earth is extremely remote and has little to do with their everyday approach to life. Most people simply do not yet see visions or remember any astral travel. But these were things which for Jimi were part of his personal world. In an interview published in a June 1969 issue of the *San Diego Free Press* he said: "I see miracles every day now. I used to be aware of them maybe once or twice a week, but some are so drastic that I couldn't explain them to a person or I'd probably be locked up by this time."

This was precisely Jimi's dilemma. He was fully aware that most others did not see the things he saw: namely, visions and astral experiences. But without these "miracles", his music and lyrics, and Jimi himself, would have been very different. One can't understand Jimi unless this is taken into account. So many of his words and statements can be read both very personally and universally. But some songs were more personal than others. It is only natural that listeners, readers and critics interpret Jimi's art through their own minds, but they must be aware that he most definitely saw different meanings behind his symbolism from those they saw.

Jimi told me that he thought his lyrics could make an important contribution to solving mankind's problems, trying to give answers, rather than just complaining. (He never found it enough to protest against evils and air grievances – as was fashionable in the 1960s – but deemed it necessary to find exact and proper answers to our world's problems, to name them, analyse them, and then start tackling them.)

It would mean missing out on the spectrum of Jimi's writing to reduce it to song lyrics. He was overflowing with all kinds of ideas, sometimes philosophizing about the nature of the world we live in, and the one we do not live in, as well as the meaning of existence in general.

He also prepared numerous projects or partial projects on paper, including ideas for a film script and plans for videos. As he had no illusions about the fact that many of his fans did not fully understand his songs and the meaning of his lyrics, Jimi planned to write a script for a video for each of his songs, giving interpretations of the meanings and messages he was so eager to convey. In the last two years of his life, from 1968, he increasingly felt that his music was largely misunderstood because of the distorted public image that had been projected by the press and his manager.

POWER OF SOUL

Here Jimi is writing, inside a crystal ball. Out of nowhere in the crystal ball a script appears in a bright focus of light. I tried to capture an event in the past, when Jimi was still here on earth, inspired by an idea which he wrote down.

The crystal ball represents a focal point, which you can use to draw powers towards yourself. It can help you to open up and allow your own inner powers to emerge. It can focus your mental energies, working like a window giving a glimpse into other dimensions. So the crystal ball can be used to help you to tune yourself into events of the past, present and future. Jimi pointed out to me that it was also possible to see all of this with your "third eye" alone, without any aid such as a crystal ball.

Jimi and I often discussed the inner powers with which so many people are gifted, but which so often lie dormant.

Jimi looked on each talent as a gift, a certain power within you. Many people have specific talents, but often are not aware of them. They may not let them emerge, or they block them out because these talents do not seem to fit in with their lifestyle, or are simply too confusing. Jimi believed that most people limit themselves, not realizing the great talents and powers they might possess. "If only people would take more of a true

"There must be so much more that people don't understand yet. At the moment, people only use a minute part of their mind and there's so much more scope. If only people wouldn't concentrate on superficial things, they might find the real meaning and true happiness…"

INTERVIEW WITH VALERIE MABBS, *RECORD MIRROR*, MARCH 1969

view, and think in terms of feelings. Your name doesn't mean a damn, it's your talent and feelings that matter." (Interview with Ritchie Yorke, *Hit Parade*, January 1970) We only use the minimum of our potential, he felt, and consequently become disenchanted with life.

When I asked Jimi what powers he was referring to, he pointed out that there are many different powers in every person. Then he asked me if I was aware that we have five physical senses, but that there are more senses in existence. Altogether, he believed, there are nine senses, although he said that so far, of these additional senses, the human race has only been able to achieve awareness of the seventh sense.

He explained that at present mankind is in the stage of the fifth sense, but evolving into the sixth. According to Jimi, someone who has gained the seventh sense through his psychic evolution has been given the power through God to understand the laws of cause and effect which govern the universe.

When I asked Jimi to tell me about the sixth sense he explained that the five senses are: touch, smell, taste, sight and hearing on the physical plane. The sixth sense enables us to see into other dimensions, including the astral plane. Jimi called this sense "free soul", because by developing it your spirit is freed and becomes active. Once you have started to do so, there are no limits. You have opened the door to your psychic powers.

Jimi added that he had tried to touch on this subject in his song "Power Of Soul":

When I told Jimi that I had not heard of the third eye, he pointed his index finger at the middle of his forehead and explained that it was located behind there. When you see a vision, according to Jimi, it appears as if you see it through your physical eyes, but in reality you see an image with the inner spiritual eye, through which we can behold visions from the past, present and future. It is part of our spirit and works on a higher plane than the normal earth level. It can see through matter and detect hidden things, like transfigurations or auras of people, sometimes even spirits and events from the other world – the Spiritworld.

He said that this power is called clairvoyance, and he believed that many people are born with this

With the power of soul,
anything is possible,
With the power of you,
anything you wanna do.

talent, but only a few come to realize it.

Another power that Jimi described is known as clairaudience – the ability to hear the "other side". Every truly inspired musician has this ability to some degree, hearing sounds from other dimensions. Some people can also sense when spirits are around and can feel if they are being touched by them. If you work on these powers they will grow within you, until it is possible to pick up the vibrations coming from the future or the past. In this way a person who is clairvoyant can receive premonitions about important events in the future.

One can even have visions of past incarnations. I had not known any of this, and I was spellbound listening to Jimi, wanting to hear more. His explanations came out so naturally that I could

sense how deeply he believed in what he said. He told me that he had seen some of his former incarnations through an astral experience, but asked me not to talk about it.

I was bewildered by what I heard. This was a theme which was to occur quite often in our discussions and this knowledge was also one of the keys to why Jimi was so universally talented. He was also able to tune in to his inner knowledge from previous existences. This also explained why he had the wisdom of a philosopher, even though he was only in his mid-twenties.

Jimi asked me if I had realized that many people only believe in what they can see with their physical eyes – yet they believe in atoms without being able to see them, because they have been scientifically proven to exist.

There are so many things, Jimi said, that scientists have yet to recognize, and which are waiting to be discovered.

He also discussed the gift of healing with me, explaining that this power cannot be seen but is nevertheless very effective. Scientists, according to Jimi, often look upon spirit healers as fakes and superstitious charlatans. They would probably consider Jesus to be one too, because he too healed others without being a doctor.

Jimi believed that Jesus was trying to teach us what incredible powers can be awakened by faith. He was sure that people would realize the truth of what he had told me, changing their attitudes in the future, when more seemingly invisible things are discovered and made accessible to the physical world.

With the power of soul anything is possible, With the power of you, anything you wanna do.

Here the power of the subconscious is opening up towards the sky, while at the same time being reflected in the waters of the sea. As the sky is our spiritual home, and the ocean the natural source of all life on earth, they can be seen as the two complementary sides of our existence: Nature and Spirit. Jimi was strongly in tune with both elements, receptive to the world around him as well as to his subconscious powers, thus having access to answers that most people would not find in a lifetime. As Jimi wrote in "Earth Blues":

My head in the clouds, my feet on the pavement.

HARMONY

Very early in our relationship Jimi told me how important it was for each person to search for and find Harmony, Inner Peace and Love, both within ourselves and on behalf of others.

In this painting, Harmony is symbolized by the dance of the different movements and combinations of colour complementing each other. A white dove, representing Peace, is emerging out of these harmonizing colours and hovering above Jimi's head. Jimi is holding a red rose in his hand which is almost invisible, but the power of love it represents is everlasting. He is playing the guitar, maybe a lyrical song like "Drifting", trying to create the vibrations of Harmony.

Jimi explained to me in 1969 that one way of finding Harmony and Inner Peace is through meditation. Another way, according to Jimi, is through music. With his music, he said, he wanted to help people find these positive emotions in themselves.

In 1968 he had already been trying to use his music as a device to bring Harmony, Peace and Love to others. "You've got to have love in your heart and try to spread it around." (Interview with Chris Welch, *Melody Maker*, January 1969)

As time progressed he intensified his mission to create clear, positive music which produced a harmonizing effect. Through the power of his music he tried to bring about fundamental changes in people's minds. He explained to me that he was aiming for a kind of awakening state, creating a higher level of thinking and evoking positive energy. At the same time he wanted to give people, especially young people, the opportunity to release aggressive, negative emotions, making them evaporate into thin air.

Jimi hoped to move people away from cynicism and bitterness, leading them towards compassion and love. In his song "Earth Blues" he says:

Lord, there's got to be some changes
Living together's gonna be a lot of rearranges
You better be ready, Lord
Let's hope love comes before the summer

Everybody, got to feel the light
Got to feel the light, baby
Everybody, got to live together
Keep it right together, right on together.

At Woodstock in 1969 he called his music "Sky Church Music", expressing clearly how he saw his spiritual and musical destiny. For Jimi everything had a deeper meaning and purpose. He was more than just a musician. He was a messenger: "It's more than music. It's like church, like a fountain for the potentially lost. We are making music into a new kind of Bible, a Bible you can carry in your heart."

THE MUSICIAN

"**A** musician, if he's a messenger, is like a child who hasn't been handled too many times by man, hasn't had too many fingerprints across his brain. That's why music is so much heavier than anything you ever felt." (Jimi Hendrix, *Life* magazine, April 1969)

In spite of all the emotional and circumstantial turmoil of his career, Jimi's playing steadily improved alongside his general musicianship. The year 1968 saw not only the peak period of his band the Experience, but also a flowering of his lead-guitar technique, his sound-painting and his songwriting.

In 1966-7 he had mainly employed his lead guitar in a less intricate and less dominant way, except in a few songs like "Bold as Love" and "Red House". But in 1968 he developed a completely new style, which grew from the roots of his original solos but took his standards much further. Before, he had treated his guitar mainly as a rhythm accompanying instrument, albeit in a truly ingenious fashion. His lead guitar had often rather served the purpose of adding colour to or supplementing vocals, rounding off his songs. Solos had been fairly short, and, up to this point, often rough and mainly blues-based.

After a while Jimi discovered that he could get more out of the guitar by concentrating on his lead playing and improving it, without of course losing his perfectly balanced and driving rhythm playing.

Other players might have been satisfied with what Jimi had achieved at that time. But for Jimi, nothing was so good that it couldn't be improved on by experimenting and exploring. He started to improvise, trying to surpass the songs he was already playing. At times this didn't work out, but when it did the results were something special. Those were the moments when Jimi and the Experience carried everyone away aboard their "spaceship". His guitar would then permeate the bodies and souls of those present and lift them up into the realms of entirely new experiences. He was drawn by the desire to always create something new, and because of his dislike of repetition, he began to improvise longer lead solos on stage, constantly trying out and introducing new elements. Being forced to reproduce his old material all the time, he tried to breathe new life into the old compositions and simultaneously to create something new.

Nineteen sixty-eight was the year of some of the group's finest concert appearances, but above all it was the year of what was perhaps their most important record, *Electric Ladyland*. The recording of this double album was spread over the first half of 1968, between extensive tours. It would become the third official Experience album and, apart from the subsequent *Smash Hits* compilation, was to be Jimi's last release with Mitch and Noel together.

Electric Ladyland was not a musical summary of the two previous LPs, but from Jimi's point of view a natural progression and a covering of territory which went far beyond the scope of these albums. For many, *Electric Ladyland* remains the finest and definitely the most revolutionary record produced by any artist that year.

By 1968 standards, this record was way ahead

of its time. Many of the effects have not been repeated since, especially Jimi's typically artistic guitar sounds. The record opens with what Jimi called a "sound-painting of Heaven and Earth", which was generated by slowed-down tapes of voices, pistol shots, bass drums and a lot of tape phasing. It also starts with frightening thunderclaps and stratospheric sounds. Slowed-down voices from outer space emerge, generating the sensation of a true time shift.

While Jimi was planning or playing a song, he would see detailed pictures and stories in his mind that he would transform into music. Jimi said he often "saw" first what he later interpreted in his songs. He had the ability to play something forwards, knowing exactly how it would sound when played back in reverse.

When playing he tried to capture what he experienced around him in the natural world. He told me that once, while in California, he was sitting alone on the seashore. He watched the evening waves of the Pacific, tuning himself in to the magical sounds of the ebbing and flowing water. He would take in a single wave, and then the waves as a unity. He imagined how each wave was formed by countless elements and forces, following the waves with his eyes and mentally slipping inside them. He recognized the interconnection between them and the steady flow of power. While watching he heard his guitar inside his head – shaping waves, building them up from calm, increasing the tension, then mounting higher and higher up to the final gigantic collapse of a crest in a sonic as well as a spiritual form.

Jimi was not the first artist to be entranced by nature. But he discovered all this for himself, by watching and comparing with his inner sources the pictures and impressions coming from outside. A

good example is "Voodoo Child (slight return)", which is full of volcanic eruptions, flights through the stratosphere and other natural phenomena. Perhaps no other musical artist of this century has visualized and translated natural principles and elements into music in such a forceful way.

In fact, Jimi's guitar-playing was mainly based on principles which he saw and felt in nature and beyond. One of the main principles which he first subconsciously and later consciously employed was never to repeat himself – for it is one of nature's first laws always to change, to keep flowing and moving forward, never standing still.

The extended "Voodoo Chile" provides another good example of Jimi's inventive guitar work. The whole song is built on a simple, almost primitive blues riff. However, what Jimi gets out of this blues-inspired idea and how he transforms it is amazing. From the very beginning he builds up a magical atmosphere which lasts until the final note of the song.

This song contains some of Jimi's most remarkable guitar-playing, spiralling upwards and downwards, crying, wailing and finally howling. At the end Jimi sings, "I have a humming bird and it hums so loud, you think you were losing your mind." He immediately proves this by improvising another great solo, for his "humming bird" is his Stratocaster guitar. At other times his guitar would burst into sheer energy and power. In his music you can feel the whole spectrum of his emotions, from loneliness to happiness, and anything in between, painting pictures of his emotional life as well as his visions and dreams. Jimi's guitar became a part of his body and soul.

When he was playing, Jimi's whole body breathed the rhythm of the song and his ability to play perfect rubato or heavy, funky swing could

"When you hear somebody making music, they are baring a naked part of their soul to you."

perhaps be partially attributed to his being of mixed race. He possessed the total rhythmic security of the black race, as well as the soft, tender and flexible streak of the white race – and not forgetting, of course, the influence of North American Indian music. Jimi blended it all into one.

His feeling for and execution of rhythm were unique. For example, his rubato playing was shown most strongly and is absolutely unsurpassed in his solo in "Machine Gun" on the *Band Of Gypsys* album, in both "Voodoo Chile" and "Voodoo Child (slight return)", as well as in "House Burning Down" and many of his live performances.

All this was entirely original Jimi, and as he pointed out to me, owed recognition to nature and the spirits who helped and inspired him. "When you hear somebody making music, they are baring a naked part of their soul to you." (Interview with Ritchie Yorke, *Hit Parade*, January 1970)

Jimi encountered difficulties in the studio because of his desire for perfection, which developed rapidly and steadily increased. He would spend precious hours, even days, getting sounds right, and would sometimes achieve only minor improvements to anyone else's ears but his own. This was an aspect of his behaviour which could infuriate some of his musicians, and also Chas Chandler, who had been his producer until Jimi took over and produced most of *Electric Ladyland* himself.

Jimi tried hard to go beyond the limits of stereophonic recording. Stereo was not enough for him: he wanted music to come from all sides, from back and front, above and below. Jimi made his guitar his voice – and not only in a figurative sense. In some of his songs, by using a wah-wah pedal, he communicates with us in an intriguing way, giving the impression that he is actually speaking to us.

Led by nothing but his own conception of what he wanted to sound like, Jimi was able to employ this, by today's standards, rather primitive device in a sensitive and unique way.

However, in speaking to us with his guitar and music, Jimi conveys not just words but also emotions, painting pictures in our minds, taking us to other dimensions, places and times, wanting us to join him on his path to higher awareness.

He kept saying that he felt he was just at the beginning of what he had to do. But in my opinion, what he achieved as a musician and a composer in his last three and a half years is remarkable. In this sense, his death transcends personal tragedy. There was so much more he wanted to give, so much more to achieve as an artist, a man, and a thinking human being.

There have been rumours that Jimi's work was deteriorating artistically during his last year. This is far from the truth: he was on the brink of a big innovative breakthrough in his music. From what he explained to me, and judging by his interviews and other statements of the time, we would soon have been able to see an altogether different Jimi. Unfortunately he was not given the time to complete this transition, the outcome of which I am sure would have been remarkable and even more exceptional than anything he had achieved so far.

In an interview with Sue Clark in December 1969, Jimi said:"I'm workin' on music to be completely, utterly magic science, where it's all pure positive. It can't work if it's not positive. The more doubts and negatives you knock out of anything, the heavier it gets and the clearer it gets. And the deeper it gets into whoever's around it. It gets contagious."

"I'm workin' on music to be completely, utterly magic science, where it's all pure positive."

A U R A S

The inspiration for this painting came to me one day as I was remembering a discussion Jimi and I had about the aura which surrounds every person, and which even surrounds planets in space.

The planet in my painting is imaginary, although it could perhaps exist somewhere in our galaxy. It is surrounded by very strong and vivid aura colours, indicating that it is a powerful planet. Jimi is standing in front of it, because he was the one who revealed the knowledge about auras to me.

When we first talked about the subject, he explained that people who have developed a sixth sense are able to see what the physical eye cannot see – an aura surrounding each human being. Jimi told me that at certain times, if he concentrated, he could see a person's aura.

The aura is the light which radiates from a person's spirit. The more active and evolved a spirit, the stronger its aura shines. Everyone has a different aura, containing a different mix of colours. The aura reflects the individual level of spiritual evolution of a person. It also indicates a person's talents and powers. The highest colour is gold, or a white which passes description. Both these colours were used by artists in the past to depict the auras of Jesus and the saints. By contrast, an evil person's aura has different shades of dull grey or black.

In between the light and the dark colours are all the others, each colour and each shade of a colour having its own specific meaning. The mixtures of these colours can reveal a lot about a person to those who are able to see the aura and have the appropriate knowledge.

As the subject fascinated me, I asked Jimi for more details, including the meaning of each colour, and asked if I could write them down. Later on he also pointed out that each planet in the sky is surrounded by an aura. These auras only reflect the purely spiritual aspects of the planets, not the material ones, which manifest themselves in a different way. Like each spirit, each planet has its own aura, and this represents a radiation of its powers. The most powerful and spiritual planet in our solar system is Jupiter, whereas Saturn possesses the strongest destructive and negative powers.

Jimi explained to me that when he was experiencing astral travel he had seen the auras of the planets which he described.

The aura reflects the individual level of spiritual evolution of a person.

Beam Me Up, Jupiter

Saturn is shaking am I going too?
Ancient powers say, "more human progress"
Friends of Earth your Peace has to enter
My blessings for you will come later

In all your strength and splendor
Do you hear my knocking?
I come running home to you Jupiter

Do you hear me knocking at your door?
People here don't want me anymore
Got to be the sad note of my song
Your inspiration is lost for so long

In all your strength and splendor
Do you hear my knocking?
I come running home to you Jupiter

Been searching this cloudy mind
For a lotus flower to find
The hidden light her secrets tell
Then out of my dreams she fell

In all your strength and splendor
Do you hear my knocking?
I come running home to you Jupiter

Within her art is a blessing
Inner creation giving our message
Fulfillment contentment and devotion
Her tender Love so full of emotion

In all your strength and splendor
Do you hear me knocking?
I come running home to you Jupiter

JIMI HENDRIX, 1970. DEDICATED TO MONIKA

BOB DYLAN'S "CHIMES OF FREEDOM"

The year 1965 brought an unexpected artistic eye-opener for Jimi. So far, his main concern had been his musical progress, with the quality of his lyrics taking second place. Until then there had simply been few songs with truly meaningful lyrics. The fashion had been for easygoing songs about love, or lightweight topics.

This was to change dramatically when Bob Dylan emerged from the folk music/protest movement and burst on to the larger music scene: an artist who was to become the finest and most influential lyricist of the sixties generation. The superior quality of his poetry and songs had first become apparent with his second album, *The Freewheelin' Bob Dylan*, released in 1963. Among others, it contained gems like "Blowin' In The Wind", "A Hard Rain's A-Gonna Fall" and "Don't Think Twice, It's Alright". This promise was to be confirmed by the two albums Dylan released in 1964, *The Times They Are A-Changing* and *Another Side Of Bob Dylan*.

By then everyone in New York's Greenwich Village who was into folk music knew about Bob Dylan. And his output didn't decrease. In 1965 he brought out two further revolutionary albums, *Bringing It All Back Home* and *Highway 61 Revisited*. The first included groundbreaking songs like "Mr Tambourine Man", "It's All Right, Ma (I'm Only

Bleeding)", the visionary "Gates Of Eden" and the hauntingly beautiful "It's All Over Now, Baby Blue". Dylan's second 1965 album contained the unique "Like A Rolling Stone", which Jimi was to perform with the early Experience a year later.

Dylan had become a star, in the process changing practically the whole face of popular music. Among his admirers were important musical figures like the Beatles, but others also came under the spell of the former protest singer with his compelling and rasping voice. Although many described Dylan's singing as "croaking", and he was quite often out of tune or out of time, his voice never lacked conviction or authority.

Like many others, Jimi recognized in Dylan a superior artist who was not only worthy of attention, but also someone from whom he could learn a great deal. Never having been too confident of his vocal abilities, Jimi realized through listening to Dylan that it was not the actual quality of the voice that mattered, but the feeling it expressed.

After his encounter with the phenomenon of Bob Dylan, Jimi's approach to songwriting would likewise never be the same again. Having been exposed in particular to the impact of Dylan's fantastic poetry, Jimi radically changed his attitude towards lyric writing. He told me that the main lesson Dylan had taught him was that poetic emotional landscapes could be painted not only with music, but also with lyrics. Dylan made Jimi realize also that young people were eager to hear serious songs with a meaning to them – not just entertaining love songs, but something that made you think.

Dylan activated something in Jimi: a compulsion which made him leave Harlem and move to Greenwich Village, to be part of a more artistic and bohemian world, with more like-

minded and free people.

Although Jimi's lyrics never became as organized, polished or perfectly timed as Dylan's, they had just as much depth and meaning in their rough but ingenious simplicity and their lyrical, fairy-tale beauty. Jimi would not sit for hours polishing his writing, but rather leave his original inspiration large untouched, just the way it came to him. He was inspired enough to have lyrics of the finest quality finished in no time at all, just as some of his greatest music came to him with equal ease.

Bob and Jimi had the visionary touch – both in their way were prophets. But while Jimi became more and more conscious of it, Dylan would shy away from such responsibilities, at least in his public statements. Dylan was a master of understatement, thus confusing those around him, and perhaps himself. His answers sometimes revealed that he was trying to maintain a protective wall around his sensitive, vulnerable nature.

For *New Musical Express* in March 1969, John Grant asked Jimi, "Is it less satisfying for you to interpret someone else's song than your own – 'All Along The Watchtower', for example?" Jimi explained, " I felt like 'Watchtower' was something I had written but could never get together. I often feel like that about Dylan. Every time I perform his 'Rolling Stone' it makes me feel so good – as though I had taken something off my mind."

In another interview, with Peter Goodman for *Beat Instrumental*, Jimi said, "Sometimes I do a Dylan song and it seems to fit me so right as a singer, not only in the early days, but then I start listening to the lyrics. That sold me."

Jimi made me see that he had sensed right from the beginning, when he first listened to Dylan's songs, a closeness in spirit to him, feeling him to be a brother, with a spiritual bond of a very

"I base my singing on real feelings and true thoughts. I learnt that from listening to Dylan."

INTERVIEW WITH JOHN GRANT, *NEW MUSICAL EXPRESS*, 1969

special kind seeming to connect them.

There was also hope in Dylan's apocalyptic vision. However, Jimi, although not an outright "political" singer, was maybe even more decisive in his quest to activate, through the power of his music, a new way of living and thinking on earth.

In August 1970 Jimi told me that one of his future plans – when the time was right – would be to join Dylan and others in order to start some kind of movement, collaborating to help transform this world into a better place.

STAR SPANGLED BANNER

The idea for this painting came to me while listening to Jimi's interpretation of the "Star Spangled Banner", which he played at the Woodstock Festival in August 1969. At that time he called his music "Sky Church Music".

In this piece Jimi expressed musically the burning of the American flag. I tried to reflect this in my painting. I painted three white lilies in the sky: the lily represents love and tenderness and makes a connection between love on earth and the Spiritworld, while the number three symbolizes strength and the chance of a breakthrough. Together the lilies stand for the hopeful rising of a more spiritual way of life for the American nation and the world in the future.

It was a very special message that Jimi intended to give to the Woodstock generation: a message that was designed to make them think about the kind of society in which they grew up – a society they themselves would one day inherit. Jimi wanted to open their eyes and make them look at reality – to realize what was going on in the world and behind the public façade of smiles and handshakes.

Jimi had already made similar statements in "House Burning Down", "I Don't Live Today", "Stone Free" and other songs. But those statements had been more or less artistically concealed and, by the use of subtle symbolism and imagery, avoided blunt confrontation.

At Woodstock Jimi made his most direct, most shocking political statement to the public. It was a severe attack on the Establishment, but also on those who just watched and complained without becoming active. Here was this tune, cherished as the sacred musical symbol of American integrity, the ideals of human rights, equality and liberty; the pride of American liberalism and nationalism; the national anthem of the United States of America: the "Star Spangled Banner". And here too was this idol of a generation, just standing there and playing guitar, attacking the national anthem in a way no one had ever dared.

Jimi started playing the melody quite in keeping with the original. Then suddenly he broke out, tearing it to pieces by introducing sounds of raging warfare, of rockets and incoming artillery shells, explosions, and the anguished cries of people caught in the terror of conflict.

He explained to me later that he was not only pointing at the Vietnam war and indeed any other war outside America, but also at the daily war which was being fought on the streets of the USA, and even in the heads of the people. He intended to show what a farce the superficially smiling face of modern society had become.

However, to avoid any misunderstanding, it should be stressed that Jimi's message was not, "Go and burn the American flag." Instead he wanted to document his own and his generation's displeasure and disappointment with the state of his country and the whole world. He explained to me that he wanted to say, "Look what is being done under the flag of freedom and justice! This is what things are really like when they are seen stripped naked. Let us all be honest and strong enough to face the facts, seriously rethink, and try together for a new beginning."

Quite apart from the political implications, I feel that Jimi was one of the few artists who actually managed to mould the chaos he saw around him into a fascinating piece of art.

"Look what is being done under the flag of freedom and justice!"

CASCADES

This painting shows Jimi in cascades of colours, representing his view that music — every note, in fact — gives out not only a certain sound but also a colour. In 1967 Jimi already saw his sounds in terms of colours, especially when he wanted to describe subtle shadings of sound. "I want to get colour into music — I'd like to play a note and have it come out a colour." (Interview with Hugh Nolan, *Disc and Music Echo*, April 1967)

He had realized that colours could express emotions, and incorporated this in some of his lyrics, the best example being "Bold As Love" from his album *Axis: Bold As Love*: "Anger he smiles, towering in shiny metallic purple armour, Queen Jealousy, Envy, waits behind him." The explanation Jimi gave me for these first two lines of the song I would like to share with you. In this book I occasionally include interpretations of lyrics which Jimi gave me, in order to show the meaning and the depth of some of his songs.

Here Jimi depicts Anger as a knight in shining metallic purple armour. By this he tried to show that Evil can adopt a disguise, wearing a smile and camouflaged with the positive colour of purple. However, this purple will never be truly spiritual, but cold and metallic — which is how it can be distinguished from its positive counterpart. Armour here generally means disguise — hiding the truth under a shining surface. Anger represents the active Evil, while Queen Jealousy, who is enviously waiting behind the knight, stands for a passive, negative force.

In another song, "The Wind Cries Mary", Jimi sings, "The traffic lights they turn blue tomorrow". Here Jimi said he was trying to describe a broken relationship he had had, and the traffic lights turning blue symbolize the kind of sadness you feel when this happens. Once again he was describing an emotion in terms of a colour.

However, you should listen to Jimi's lyrics yourself. For instance, I have referred to only the first two lines of "Bold As Love", but the whole song is all about colours and their metaphysical meanings. Although the main theme is love, everything is expressed by means of colour. Jimi goes through the spectrum: green, blue, turquoise, red, orange and so on, releasing a whole cascade of explanations and allusions, giving a clear insight into his philosophy of colours and how he connects them with certain emotions and ideas. Later, in 1969, Jimi talked to me again about his interest in

"I want to get colour into music — I'd like to play a note and have it come out a colour."

"Anger he smiles, towering in shiny metallic purple armour, Queen Jealousy, Envy, waits behind him."

the relationship between music and colour. In fact he was trying to discover which colours correspond to which musical notes by finding the key to a knowledge which he believed had been lost for a long time, since the days of Atlantis.

He knew, as is now being confirmed by experts, that each sound and each colour emits some specific wave patterns, analogous to different states of the human psyche. Certain sounds as well as colours are able to reharmonize confused physical and psychic conditions. Others can have a depressive effect on people, bringing out negative emotions.

Thus, Jimi believed, if you chose the right sounds, they could put you into different states of mind, by making you more receptive to different kinds of vibrations and emotions – ranging from love and harmony to hate and destruction. This is the reason why Jimi believed that music is magic – a supernatural power. He explained to me that he saw his musical work as a magic science, where everything was meant to be purely positive. Moreover, it could only work if it was positive. According to Jimi, the more you knock the negative out of everything, the stronger the effect of the music and the more it will touch the human soul.

Jimi also believed that rhythm could become hypnotic – putting the hearer in a trance-like condition – if you repeated it over and over again. All life follows rhythmic patterns – be it day and night, birth and death, or the pulse in our bodies. Rhythm opens people up by activating and releasing their own rhythmic roots. The peoples of many cultures – for example those of Africa or the North American Indians – use this power of repeating certain rhythms to put themselves into a different, more dynamic and flowing state of mind, which can also have a healing effect.

But to Jimi the healing power of music was not restricted to some people alone, but could be used on a global scale, because music is a universal language. He was well aware that at very big events like rock concerts, massive energies could be gathered and channelled in either a good or a destructive way, depending on the nature of the music being played.

One of Jimi's plans for the future was to compose special songs with a concentration of certain notes in them – to bring out the positive side of people, or just give them more harmony and peace of mind. He explained to me that he was aiming to play pure, positive music, thus healing people's minds and enabling them to change the world into a better place.

In the last year of his life Jimi concentrated his efforts on composing songs which brought out positive energy. He also suggested to other people besides me that he would like to play a different kind of music – rock, but "happy rock". "I'd like to write symphonies that take you somewhere – sight and sound together creating a new sense." (Interview with Bob Partridge, *Record Mirror*, September 1970)

Jimi felt that there was still so much to be discovered in this field and I know he wanted me to go into the subject more deeply. However, in the summer of 1970 he told me that, following certain spiritual experiences, he had found answers to some key questions. He had set up a complete scale, assigning the right colours to the right musical notes, and he explained these correspondences to me in great detail. I was so fascinated by his discovery that I wrote them all down straight away.

"The traffic lights they turn blue tomorrow"

SPARKS OF CREATIVITY

Creativity is a key concept in understanding Jimi's life and work. This painting shows him surrounded by sparks of creativity. Everyone, he believed, could have access to their creative potential, if they would only open up the creative side of their being and not impose artificial limits on themselves.

Jimi explained to me that this was one important point which he was trying to get across. He wanted people to activate their creativity, and wished we could just remember what we felt deep inside when we were children, before society imprinted our minds with labels and filled our heads with useless, often negative information. Children, he believed, were able to feel and think in an intuitive and natural way, being open to a free flow of inspiration. This, in particular, is something most of us lose as we are formed and educated according to the demands of society.

In Jimi's opinion school does not teach us how to use our senses and command our minds in order to find inner knowledge and creative resources. On the contrary, it helps prepare people to put on uniforms and lock themselves away in cages, so that, when they are older, it becomes almost impossible to break out. Jimi said to me, "Subconsciously people are killing off all these little flashes they have." I can remember Jimi speaking with passion and conviction on this theme, which

he considered to be vital for the individual's, and also mankind's, development. A person's creative flashes, according to Jimi, indicate his or her spirit's activity. The societies of today tend to suppress all the creative sparks and flashes a person might have. But people themselves also tend to ignore them, because they do not understand what they mean.

Find yourself first
And then your tool
Find yourself first
Don't you be no fool.

Jimi says in the song "Messages To Love". Later in this song he emphasizes:

I said find yourself first
And then your talent
Work hard in your mind
And it will come alive!

Jimi told me that in this song he had tried to express the importance of finding yourself and discovering the inner source in your spirit. Once this gate has been opened, you will feel like a person reborn. Your talents, locked away for such a long time, will start to break free. All of a sudden you will know who you are, realizing your purpose in life and your true potential, which has been buried in yourself for so long.

Everyone, Jimi told me, is master of his own destiny: it is necessary to find your spirit and awaken it. Otherwise you will walk around like a zombie, living a life of errors and illusions, a life of

"I don't know what's happening in England, but the dollar bill is God in the States. All those pelican people just believe in money and nothing else."

INTERVIEW WITH CHRIS WELCH, *MELODY MAKER*, JANUARY 1969

emptiness with no access to your true purpose and meaning, enslaved in a materialistic world.

Jimi believed that the most important step and task in life is to free yourself from materialistic thinking. The less you are captured by this trap, the easier it is to find the creative powers enclosed within. Once you have broken the chains that have trapped you since childhood, you will be free and you will see your life in a different, much clearer light.

Jimi warned me that this route is not easy and it may call for many sacrifices. It all depends, he said, on how deeply you want to explore your purpose in life. The deeper you go, the more sacrifices you will have to make. It will certainly become more difficult, but you will also be able to see everything with more clarity.

He told me that he felt he had to make a lot of sacrifices in his own life, including his private life, in order to do what he was meant to do. He had dedicated himself to his music and the messages it held, knowing that to create something truly worthwhile, not only is a great deal of love and faith necessary, but also the understanding that you must make sacrifices.

Jimi believed that once you are creative in a genuine way you are getting closer to your own heaven. To create is to move towards the Light of the Lord, the Creator, whose creative spark is in all of us, and is the basis of our inspiration as artists and human beings.

You are what you are Thank God
You Gonna Shine like a Star
with the help of God -
But we find our selfs first
2and then our tool ...
Find your self first dont be no
fool

MACHINE GUN

- - - - - - -

Yeah. Machine Gun tearing my family apart,

Yeah, yeah, tearing my family apart.

I sincerely share Jimi's belief that the solution to the problems of this world cannot be found through war, but only through love. In this picture you see Jimi with his guitar, screaming out against the madness of war, empathizing with all the pain, suffering and agony that come with it. In the sky you see attacking fighter planes, dropping bombs of destruction, killing innocent people on the ground, heedless of whether they are old, women, children or babies. Fireballs from explosions are scattered around, and the sky is bathed in grey – the colour of evil. This is a place of hell.

In the foreground are three young men, little more than children, holding machine guns, shooting and killing other young men, who in the eyes of God are equally his children. Thus in every war brother is killing brother, without in most cases even being aware of it. In fact, all wars would come to an end if people would open their hearts and eyes and recognize one another as a brother or sister – a fellow soul.

Jimi was strongly against war, violence and aggression. He knew that warfare was not supplying the world with any answers to its problems, however grave these were. Although he made many statements on the subject, I believe the clearest to be his song "Machine Gun", a particular version of which he played at Fillmore East in New York on 1 January 1970, and which was subsequently released on the album *Band Of Gypsys*.

In this anti-war song he not only sings against war in the true sense, but also makes the whole band, and especially his guitar, a war machine, recreating the sounds and the whole apocalyptic atmosphere of warfare. At the beginning Jimi says: "We'd like to dedicate this one to the draggin'est scene going on. All the soldiers that are fighting in Chicago and Milwaukee and in New York… Oh yes, and all the soldiers that are fighting in Vietnam!"

"The truth is straight ahead, so don't burn yourself, instead – try to learn instead of burn, hear what I

Machine Gun, yeah, tearing my body all apart
Evil man make me kill you
Evil man make you kill me
Evil man make me kill you
Even though we're only families apart.

Later he sings:
Same way you shoot me down baby
You'll be goin' away just the same three times
   the pain
And your own self to blame. Hey Machine Gun

'Cause I know all the time you're wrong baby
And you'll be going away just the same
Yeah. Machine Gun tearing my family apart,
Yeah, yeah, tearing my family apart.

After the song, having created the sounds of bombs exploding, machine guns rattling and young soldiers dying on the battlefield, he says into the microphone, "Yeah, that's what we don't want to hear any more of, right?" Then Buddy Miles, the drummer, adds, "No bullets, no guns, no bombs."

Jimi's message in this song is crystal-clear. He was not simplistic: his intention in using such basic statements was to make clear that no matter how complex and entangled a human problem war may be, it always boils down to very simple patterns in the end. He oversimplifies this message in order to show what war really is: a man-eating machine serving no one but evil.

He later told me that the idea for "Machine Gun" came to him one morning when recalling an astral travel experience he had had during the night, where he had found himself next to a dying and groaning soldier.

However, to Jimi, not every war was unjust. He was not a pacifist in the strict sense of the word. He did not say, "Do not fight at all" but he did say, "Don't fight a senseless war – make sure you know what you are doing and what you are taking part in, as you yourself are responsible for your actions." Jimi's music in "Machine Gun" and "Star Spangled Banner" is equally direct, uncompromising and shocking, and is perfectly matched by the lyrics of "Machine Gun". There is hardly a more direct or clearer way of artistically extracting and unveiling the very essence of war.

Jimi explained that he believed ultimately that not only were the leaders to blame, but also everyone who accepts what makes war possible. Even ordinary people will be held responsible, he believed, although perhaps to a lesser degree, when Karma reaches out for them, making them pay dearly for what they have taken part in, made possible, or failed to do. Specifically, Jimi believed that the pain you cause by killing someone will come back to haunt you threefold. All this and more he tried to express in "Machine Gun". In the studio, Jimi created a different version of the song by making a medley of lyrics and music from "Machine Gun" and "Izabella", which appeared posthumously years later on the album *Midnight Lightning*.

He told me that what he was trying to express in his songs was that at every moment there are terrible things going on all over the world – war, destruction and terror – and that he wanted to open people's eyes. Most of them turn a blind eye to these horrors instead of becoming actively involved in stopping them. He wanted to point a finger at the suffering of this world and make people do something to change the mistaken course pursued by mankind. War and conflict are everyday realities: man killing his fellow man, so-called leaders telling their young soldiers that the other side is the enemy. However, anyone who delves deeper should realize that we are all brothers and sisters in the eyes of the Lord.

"Don't fight a senseless war – make sure you know what you are doing and what you are taking part in, as you yourself are responsible for your actions."

Jimi explained to me the lyric of "House Burning Down", written in 1968. In it he asks, "Why do you burn your brother's house down?" As the house also symbolizes a country, he is actually asking, "Why did someone belonging to the same family, the family of mankind, destroy his or her own brother's house?" A man steps forward, shouting, "We're tired and disgusted, so we paint red through the sky." Jimi told me that this man's words express a common attitude: people, being tired and disgusted by a situation, eventually become too blind to see any other solution but painting the sky red – meaning to start war or violence. Jimi's answer to him is equally simple: "the truth is straight ahead, so don't burn yourself, instead – try to learn instead of burn, hear what I say!"

These lines contain the true answer to our dilemma. No problem is so grave that it can't be solved with faith and a positive attitude. Jimi felt no war was justified except when you are directly attacked and are forced to defend yourself, your family and friends. He believed that if we search for solutions, they are already there, straight in front of us, but we have to find them. If we search for the truth seriously and deeply, we will find it.

For our purpose on earth is to learn, not to kill or destroy. Jimi pointed out to me that there are so many ways of killing someone. People can kill and destroy each other figuratively just by words, by saying only three sentences, or even one particular word.

Jimi then explained to me more about war and people's destruction of this world.

And way down in the background
I can see frustrated souls and cities burnin'
And on across the water, baby,

I see weapons barkin' out the sting of death
And up in the clouds I can imagine UFO's
Chuckling to themselves, laughing, they sayin'
"Those people are so uptight, they sure know
how to make a mess."

These lines – from a song which was later called "Somewhere Over The Rainbow" and appeared on the album *Crash Landing* – mirror the death-bringing consequences of human aggression as seen from a higher, more objective standpoint.

Jimi told me that he had seen people in Harlem stoned, helpless and lethargic, having lost all hope, just protesting, instead of trying to change their condition or the situation within the community. He believed that you could always do something to improve matters, even if it was only on a small scale. If everyone became more active it would produce a snowball effect and things would start changing everywhere. To a certain degree, Jimi blamed the "laziness" of people for the state of the world as well, and spoke about it in some of his interviews.

He also explained that he knew from his own

And way down in the background
I can see frustrated souls and cities burnin'
And on across the water, baby,
I see weapons barkin' out the sting of death
And up in the clouds I can imagine UFO's
Chuckling to themselves, laughing, they sayin'
"Those people are so uptight, they sure know
how to make a mess."

forget of my name).. Remember it
only as a hand shake ...introduction
to my Belief which is God... Fine instead
the Waves of my Interpreture. Music, saint
Hypnotic if you choose) But Thruth and
life regardless of your questionable timid
~~peace keeping~~ compromises.. Which
I intend to erase.... Which I ~~will~~ erase
without hint of reward as I am only
a messenger And you a Sheep in process
of evolution .. Almost at Death with yourself
and On the Stair case of Birth. Soon you
may almost forget the Smell of your family ..

experience that there are inner wars to be fought: "If you start thinking negative, it switches to bitterness, aggression, hatred, whatever." He believed we should be constantly battling against all negative emotions. It seemed vital to him not to give in to those weaknesses, never letting oneself be dragged towards evil. As this inner war is an essential part of human existence, each one of us has to struggle with it all our lives – even Jesus and Buddha, as well as other holy men, had to resist the forces of evil.

So there was only one war, Jimi believed, that all of us should be taking part in – the war against evil.

"Quite naturally, you say, 'Make love not war', and all of these other things, but then you come back to reality – there are some evil folks around,

more harmony among the people and towards more peace, love, understanding and brotherhood. This is the way we have to understand some of the things he says in his song "Izabella":

You know we got this war to fight.
Hey Izabella,
I am fighting this war for the children and you
All this blood is for the world of you.

And later he says:
I can't quit till the devil's on the run.

Jimi told me that he had realized that people seem to be unaware of a permanent fight going on between good and evil in this world. Good and evil forces, he was convinced, are in conflict over the

falsehood and evil, and changing this world from a cruel place into a warm and loving one, which he tried to express in his song "Straight Ahead".

Evil – in the shape of the devil – is also a theme of "Look Over Yonder":

Lord knows we don't need
A devil like him beatin' us around
Well he's knockin' on my door
Now my house is tumblin' down
Don't you come no closer
The path is gettin' colder
Stay away from my door, baby
Unless you want to start another war.

I can't quit till the devil's on the run.

and they want you to be passive and weak and peaceful so that they can just overtake you like jelly on bread…

"You have to fight fire with fire. I mean, I'm getting myself personally together in the way of music and what I'm going to do." (Interview with Jacoba Atlas, *Circus*, March 1969)

Jimi had an utter belief in this battle against hatred, greed, corruption, crime, ignorance and discrimination – all the things evil thrives on. In this way he felt he was a warrior, fighting evil because he wanted to redirect the world towards

fate of mankind and the world. He believed that the next few decades are a crucial historical period for the destiny and future of earth and its inhabitants.

He told me that he felt that if mankind continued to follow its path of destruction, it would lead to global disaster, evil having the chance to take control of our world. He wanted everybody to take part in this fight, for only together, he felt, would mankind be able to activate both their own power and a spiritual force sufficiently strong to confront evil successfully. He wanted people to come together, join forces, fighting against

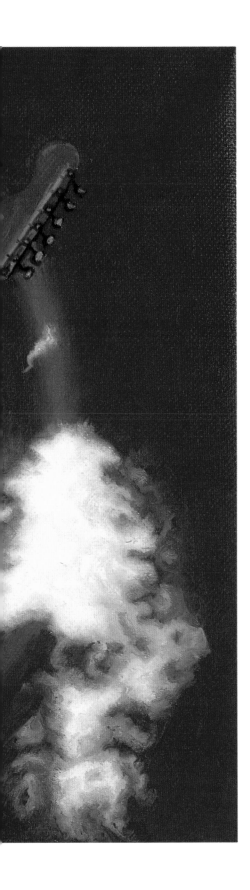

SPANISH CASTLE MAGIC

People must never be afraid of paths chosen by
   God…
In their hearts, they see the path so much more
   clearly
and truthfully than even the eyes –
But in time, the tempting beautiful body
only as far as the eyes will in time,
come to pass.
Today I burn under my brain's consciences
of what propels me out of trouble at times
into Time itself,
outside into the space of it all….
My body cannot breathe there…
What is my mind doing there?
Why is my soul surpassing
curious, egos, security, etc.,
going fast as the speed of thought –
the fastest and longest far reaching thing we know.
Long ago sleepless nights would drift in
with their bags and books of wonderments
and self debates…not of myself
but of stars, music, Saturn's rings astro-notions –
Before L.S.D. there were visions of eternities…..

so many blisters un-medicated, unraped by human
   eyes
as today on all across this earth
and through this house and home
That need not be explained to you but
to the Devil..
The truth shall be known to all….
The will to accept the truth must be fed,
never suspiciously bled.
It's just that we must prepare for one….
the amazement in how the truth shall be presented
–
Nature shows more than anything
and it does get pretty amazing –
What's sometimes more amazing is how,
people miss the warnings of tidal waves,
Volcanoes….earthquakes – etc…
I know inside they pretend to miss the message
We really could not care for our children –
How can you push it back on yourself in the long
   run –
As we feel…eventually
we shall be our own children –

FROM "THE TERRA REVOLUTION AND VENUS" BY JIMI HENDRIX

REVOLUTION OF THE MIND

Here Jimi is gazing and pointing at the onlooker, telling him or her to go forward and break through the cobwebs of yesterday's thinking.

His belief was that as well as revolutionizing the outer world, we should also be examining ourselves, striving for a higher level of thinking and a clearer way of analysing and experiencing our inner world. What he was aiming for was a revolution without guns or wars – a revolution of the mind. I remember Jimi talking of his belief that there are still many people who don't give themselves a chance, not really developing either their brain or their soul.

Killing one another with war or words, he said, is the worst way to go. The key to creating a new, more just and spiritual world lies within ourselves and first has to be found. The second step for mankind should be to communicate and to become organized. However, only the power of the people can bring about these changes.

The gun Jimi is holding expresses the idea that some day this symbol of war and destruction, along with all other martial equipment, will become a relic of the past. The lotus flower in the barrel reflects Jimi's sense of humour, but also represents the seeds of great achievements in the future.

"Bullets'll be fairy tales."

"There'll be a renaissance from bad to completely clear and pure and good – from lost to found."

INTERVIEW WITH ROBIN RICHMAN, *LIFE* MAGAZINE, OCTOBER 1969

VALLEYS OF NEPTUNE — ARISING

This painting shows Jimi in front of a setting he once described to me as a vision he had had — a vision he also portrayed in a song called "Valleys Of Neptune — Arising". This song does not refer to the planet Neptune, but to a sunken island kingdom in the Atlantic Ocean — the legendary Atlantis.

Jimi stands in the foreground, playing his guitar to a celestially illuminated dawn. In the background, on the burning edge "arising", are the newborn mountains of Atlantis — just having emerged from the ocean.

Neptune is the Roman god of the sea. Jimi also saw a time of destruction like a global deluge approaching for our world. The deluge he foresaw need not necessarily be taken literally. It is meant to be a metaphor for an event swallowing up all the wrong and evil ways of our world, so that a spiritually reborn world may rise and take its place. Although this version of the song was never published, it contains some of Jimi's most beautiful lyrics.

The painting shows the rising sun just coming

Singing about the Valley of Sunsets,
Green and Blue Canyons too,
Singing 'bout Atlantis love songs,
The Valleys of Neptune is arising.

Singing about the Valley of Sunsets,
Purple and gold,
Home of the Armies of the Lord,
Singing about Ancient Moon trips,
The Valleys of Neptune is arising.

out, and a new world – like Atlantis used to be – emerging from the ocean. Through his songs, Jimi intended to prepare people for an awakening and a new beginning: a new world, which he also called the "Land of the New Rising Sun".

This prediction, the motif of a new world taking the place of an old, worn-out one, keeps recurring in many of Jimi's songs – for example "Hey Baby (The Land Of The New Rising Sun)" and "Voodoo Chile (slight return)" – as well as in many of his other unpublished lyrics and in the last poem.

Most of the Atlantean population was highly evolved spiritually, but at the same time they lived simple lives.

When Jimi first talked to me about Atlantis, I knew little about the subject and asked him to tell me as much about it as possible. According to Jimi, this island existed about 10,000 years ago. In a dream he had seen that it had the shape of a rounded triangle. The inhabitants were of mixed race and looked different from people living nowadays. Most of the Atlantean population was highly evolved spiritually, yet they lived simple lives. Among them were seers who travelled around the world, imparting their enormous knowledge and wisdom.

The Atlanteans were aware of the different dimensions in the Spiritworld, and knew about good and evil planes. They were a highly talented and gifted race, who knew how to put their assets to good use. They lived in harmony within themselves, with one another and with the laws of the cosmos. Therefore, whatever they asked for, they received, because each of them was aware of his or her spiritual powers.

Even the island itself was permeated by powers. It was a magical place, full of force and energy, almost a living entity, giving out warnings through natural signs. Although not the only inhabited place on earth, Atlantis was nevertheless the most beautiful and powerful of them all. It was a world of many wonders. The main island touched the realms of heaven with its powers, like a huge mountain in the middle of the sea – spiritually in tune with other mighty forces above and beyond.

This was the "Golden Age" – almost like the Spiritworld brought down to earth. To the Atlanteans, time meant something different from what is the case nowadays. And, although their knowledge has been lost over the centuries, they were aware of and attuned to a different, absolute time, which Jimi called "Planetary Time". They also read the stars and planets and were very advanced in all such areas of knowledge. Jimi thought that they were in contact with and received visits from Galacticans from outer space.

When I asked Jimi whether the people of Atlantis were more advanced in spirit than we are

People nowadays have a lot of factual and technical information, but they lack knowledge of the things that really matter.

today, he replied that they were special – not more advanced, but stronger in powers and knowledge. Theoretically, people today might have the same potential, but they let themselves be too much distracted by materialistic concerns, whereas the Atlanteans were spiritual in a true sense, and had found the path to themselves. In Atlantis, most things were done through mental powers. People nowadays have a lot of factual and technical information, but they lack knowledge of the things that really matter.

When I wanted to know how it could be possible for such a spiritual place to perish, Jimi told me the story of the final destruction of Atlantis. It was not an atomic bomb, but a force from outer space that brought about its demise. However, before this occurred the Atlanteans were attacked from within. For a long time the political power of Atlantis had been growing stronger and stronger, until one day the soul of the race began to develop something like a cancer. Evil spirits, incarnated on earth, with the help of powerful evil forces from above, were infiltrating the island in subtle and covert ways. The Atlanteans' historic mistake was to become less cautious because of their strategic might. In their late period they were the strongest sea power, also having control over large parts of the Mediterranean. Indeed, being superior to all the other nations of the world, they came to consider themselves invincible.

As their circumspection waned, and their worldly influence continued to grow, they failed to heed the warnings they had been given. During their civilization's rise, evil had grown from within their core, and started to attack them from inside. As this power was using the force of the islanders themselves, and pitting them against one another, it rapidly grew to unforeseen size.

Thus, the Atlanteans' unity broke, despite their knowledge and awareness of the existence of evil, for they did not expect it to attack as it did – from within. Once evil had gained a footing the constructive and positive people, who could see

what had gone wrong, did not fight back effectively – very much like today. Communication between them had broken down, and evil could take control.

Now the Atlanteans changed their character, eventually threatening the whole Mediterranean with their tyranny. The island of Atlantis resembled a body destroyed by cancer, and the only release was death. Like all evil, it attracted destruction, having lost its heavenly protection. Karma came knocking at the door.

In the end, a comet hit Atlantis and its islands. Within a single day the whole archipelago had sunk into the depths of the sea. The level of all the oceans rose in an immense tidal wave, rolling over the whole planet, and resulting in a giant global catastrophe. The earth trembled, volcanoes erupted worldwide, most humans perished and whole continents changed shape.

This was what the Bible referred to as the "Great Deluge". However, some Atlanteans who had not yet yielded to the influence of the evil forces had been able to read the warnings in time. When they realized what was going to happen, they set sail for other continents. Some went to the mountains of South America, the Andes; others settled in the Himalayas, Egypt and elsewhere.

Jimi told me that in his view today's world is in a similar situation to the time of Atlantis. But it still may not be too late to avert the disaster which will inevitably follow if mankind continues to pursue its present egotistical path. I hope that our future is true to Jimi's vision of a spiritual and happy Atlantis rising again.

Atlantis was a magical place, full of force and energy, almost a living entity...

JIMI'S PROPHECY

"**B**ut like the solar system is going through a change soon and it's going to affect the Earth in about 30 years, you know… I am talking about the Earth itself." (*San Diego Free Press*, June 1969)

In the last days of his life, Jimi told me about a strong belief he held, and took a writing pad, to illustrate more clearly what he meant.

Before going into the subject, he talked for a while about a song he had written called "If Six Was Nine". He told me that there is also a cosmic meaning to that song, hidden in the two numbers six and nine. Jimi said that these numbers together are a very powerful force, and he drew them within each other. It looked like a spiral when he added more rays, the individual rays as well as the whole form spinning to the right. He said the sign with nine rays in it is the symbol of a very high spiritual power which is coming towards earth.

He was convinced that, in the near future, Galacticans from outer space, from another galaxy of great positive power, would come to our planet to help mankind in its struggle against evil. While explaining this, he drew two points representing this higher power coming closer and closer towards our galaxy, the Milky Way, finally reaching earth.

Jimi then made another sketch with four spiral rays pointing leftwards, telling me that this symbol is a negative one, because its rays point to the left.

He told me that the arrival of the positive power would bring about a great change on our planet. Love, peace and brotherhood among the peoples on earth would start to blossom again, just as they had in the ancient civilization of Atlantis. He said that the signs of the beginning of these events would be when significant unexpected changes started to happen in the world. But he also pointed out that we, the people, would also have to become active and anticipate bringing about these positive changes for ourselves and our world. He explained that people on earth have been asleep for too long and an awakening is beginning to happen to the people as this higher power approaches our world.

This prophecy of Jimi's was the inspiration for this painting. A spacecraft, one of many to follow, is approaching our galaxy, its destination planet earth.

Jimi also refers to this event in his last poem, "The Story of Life":

Angels of heaven
Flying saucers to some
Made Easter Sunday
The name of the rising sun.

GYPSY SUNSET

J imi was always in motion: he was a restless traveller, constantly moving in mind and body. Throughout his life he was searching and exploring. In typical gypsy fashion he kept moving from place to place. This is reflected in his star sign, Sagittarius, the sign of the long-distance traveller.

The sun in the painting represents the everlasting cycle of nature and all creation – birth, death and rebirth. Birds of passage are on their way, symbolizing the long journey of the soul, travelling away from the cold towards the warmer regions.

The photograph of Jimi which I used for this painting was taken during the last month of his life. As the sun goes down, Jimi's soul flies away, leaving earth to join the migration of the birds. I envisage this picture as Jimi's farewell to music and life, a farewell represented by the birds' passage to another land far away.

The sunset means "goodbye" to one world and "hello" to the next. On the night before he died, Jimi gave me his last poem, in which he says:

After I had finished this painting I realized that the negative used to print the photograph from which I was working had been reversed – so that it showed Jimi playing the guitar the wrong way round. My first response was to try to repaint the picture in reverse to correct this mistake. But then I realized that the mirror image produced a totally different atmosphere and meaning, and I much preferred my original version.

The story of life is quicker than the wink of an eye. The story of love is hello and goodbye. Until we meet again!

135

Rendezvous
in Another World

This is a part of one of Jimi's ideas for a private painting he wanted me to do. In March 1969 he asked me to paint a picture showing him asleep in one country, for example when he was on tour, while I am shown asleep in another. At the same time you would see us together on the astral plane – a thousand miles away from each other, yet at the same time together in another dimension.

Jimi was sure that when you are physically apart from your loved one your spirits could still meet and be together. He explained to me that while their physical earth bodies are asleep, the astral bodies of two people can leave them, and meet on a higher plane.

Because of Jimi's death, I changed part of his idea, instead just showing him and me meeting in the Spiritworld. He had told me that this is possible for two people, even when one of them is still living on earth, while the other has returned to Spiritland.

While their physical earth bodies are asleep, the astral bodies of two people can leave them, and meet on a higher plane.

Teardrops are turning into a waterfall, spreading life over the stars below — until they eventually dissolve into the eternal, infinite cosmic sea and a new galaxy is born. In "Drifting" Jimi sings:

Drifting on a sea of forgotten teardrops

On a lifeboat

Sailing for — your love,

Sailing home.

Four Races in One

Together with his last poem, this painting is Jimi's artistic requiem. It was the first of a series of paintings he wanted me to do in order to help him clarify and reinforce his message. Jimi often felt that he was not fully understood in his songs and especially in his lyrics, which dealt with love, peace, freedom and brotherhood. Some of these paintings were intended as interpretations of his lyrics.

His idea was that he should create sound-paintings with his music, while I created oil paintings, together showing more clearly what he wanted to express. He wished to combine our arts, hoping this would have a bigger impact and make people more aware of his message and the answers he had found to change our world into a better one.

On Thursday 17 September 1970, the day before he died, Jimi and I sat together discussing this particular painting, and he gave me detailed instructions on how I should paint it. He intended it to be used either as a record cover or, if he was able to release a double album, as an inside cover in combination with another painting. The album on which he was then working was later released as *The Cry Of Love*, but this was not the title he had in mind. In his last few days we had spoken about his forthcoming album, which he had intended to call either *Gypsy's Rainbow* or *Rock Of Ages*. He finally decided to use the second.

Jimi had been seriously upset about the cover of his previous album, *Electric Ladyland*, which had been released by the British record company with an obscene photograph that he absolutely hated. He had written to the American record company, asking them to use a selection of photographs by Linda McCartney showing the Jimi Hendrix Experience in the midst of little children. Instead, the album was released in England with nineteen naked women on the cover.

Ever since 1968 Jimi had sought to escape from his "wild man" image, which he had come more and more to recognize as a trap and a burden. Quite soon after his initial success, Jimi had grown into a mature and serious artist, but in the public eye he was still perceived as a guitar-smashing rebel. People expected him to live up to the image which had made him famous. He now wanted to take over the design and layout of his record covers, posters and photos in order to clarify his true identity.

Jimi explained his standpoint to me at length on various occasions, knowing that, as an artist, I would be more likely to understand him. When talking about this painting, he took a writing pad and began to make a sketch in order to demonstrate his idea to me. His concept was a painting of the four races of mankind in the shape of a cross, combining various portraits of different people with one of himself in the middle. The expressions on their faces were to vary so as to symbolize the multiplicity of human emotions: one face maybe happy, another sad, one serious, another maybe

indifferent. The painting, according to Jimi, was to symbolize the planet earth and its people: good and evil, lost and saved, happy and sad. In other words, it was to represent mankind.

He wished each race to be represented by several components – each arm of the cross being composed firstly of one or more prominent figures from each of the four races, and secondly of one or more women, followed by a little baby at each end. The baby, Jimi explained to me, was to symbolize the future of mankind, which can only be guaranteed through the survival and well-being of future generations.

On the left of the painting, Jimi wanted the black race: directly next to him a black woman with a crown, then Martin Luther King – a man he admired and felt close to in spirit, a man of peace – followed by two more women with different expressions on their faces, and then a baby.

Above Jimi's portrait, he wanted me to paint the yellow race. The first figure he had chosen was Buddha, the Enlightened One. After him came Genghis Khan, the Mongolian warrior-ruler of the twelfth century, who, in Jimi's eyes, was a truly evil man, having conquered and extended his empire from China to Europe's Adriatic Sea in the most brutal and horrific way. These were followed by two portraits of a Japanese woman and a Chinese woman, with a baby completing the top arm of the cross.

On the right, Jimi had planned the white race. Drawing the next face, he said he wanted the German leader Hitler next to him. In Jimi's view,

> He now wanted to take over the design and layout of his record covers, posters and photos in order to clarify his true identity.

Hitler had not originally been evil, but through weakness had opened himself to evil forces, and then he became evil himself. Jimi pointed out to me that Hitler had misused the swastika – an ancient sacred symbol – for his own low purposes, and that he had also practised black magic. Hitler's ruin, Jimi said, was predetermined, partly because he had misused a sacred symbol for evil means, and that by so doing had activated a higher power which would not permit such sacrilege to pass unpunished. Next to Hitler, he had planned John F. Kennedy, who had given young Americans so much hope. Beside Kennedy were again two women, with the baby at the end.

Beneath his own portrait, Jimi drew North American Indians – the red race. First was Geronimo, who was the Apache leader of the Chiricahua Apache tribe, and who led his people's defence of their homeland against the military force of the white man. He was also a medicine man and a prophet.

Below Geronimo came Crazy Horse, the Indian chief of the Oglala tribe. He was a most cunning tactician and a determined warrior in the Sioux resistance to the white man's invasion of the Northern Great Plains. But Crazy Horse was also a spiritual man, who claimed that to get into the real world he had to dream, and that when he was in the real world everything seemed to float and dance. He died very young while trying to escape imprisonment, although some believe he was tortured to death by the military guard.

Then Jimi drew Cochise, the Chiricahua Apache chief who led the North American Indians' resistance in the south-west of the country. Although a warrior, he believed in peace, and at a meeting with General Granger said, "I came here because God told me to do so. He said it was good

The painting was to symbolize the planet earth and its people: good and evil, lost and saved, happy and sad.

to be at peace – so I came!" However, after being deceived and wounded during talks with a white delegation, and after some of his tribesmen had been killed, Cochise laid plans to avenge the death of his friends. The warfare of his Apache bands was fierce and he and two hundred followers eluded capture for more than ten years. He later became a man of peace, still fighting passionately, but now in a peaceful way, for the freedom of his people.

Jimi pointed out that these three North American Indian chiefs were the ones who most impressed him when he learned the stories of their lives, and that each one represents different things.

He then drew two North American Indian women, and again a baby at the end. When he did this he asked me if I could do more paintings in the future based on the theme of North American Indians.

Jimi paused as he wrote "MONIKA" at the bottom of the sketch. Until then I had always signed my paintings "DAMO". My father did not approve of my being a painter, and as a protest I signed my pictures in this way, "DA" being the first two letters of my father's name, and "MO" the first two of mine. However, Jimi decided that in future I should sign my paintings "MONIKA", and I hesitantly promised to do so.

We went on talking about the so-called "Cross Painting", the final title of which is "Four Races in One". Jimi made me realize that through this painting he wanted to express the fact that all races are equal, being all brothers and sisters, the Children of God. "I don't look at things in terms of races. I look at things in terms of people." (*Music Maker*, February 1968)

Jimi asked me to emphasize the colour of each race, so that everyone would realize the contrast and the barriers which the human races had artificially created between each other. In ethnic respects, Jimi was himself completely colour-blind, realizing that all the differences between races and individuals were not representative of the core of their personalities.

After a while I started to make another sketch of the same picture, and Jimi asked me why. I explained that under no circumstances did I want Hitler to be positioned next to him, but that it should be John F. Kennedy. I asked if I could make this change, and he agreed with a smile.

He then gave me instructions to use the colour mauve for the background. Purple, the colour which unites all colours, and also symbolizes the planet Jupiter, to which he felt himself connected, was to be used for the inner circle, as well as for his portrait. The circle symbolizes Spirit. He wanted to show in the painting that all races on earth are part of the same Spiritworld, where all races are merged into one, although on earth we are born into different races. Jimi believed that in our separate incarnations we can be born into the white, black, yellow or red race. In order to make this clearer, he asked me not to use either black or white in this painting, which made it very difficult for me when I began work on it in October 1970.

Jimi's way of thinking was a universal one, yet whether in his music, his lyrics, or as now in a painting, every detail had its specific meaning.

He made it clear to me that he wanted to have every race in this painting, as he felt that he himself represented all the races. He said to me, "Never look at the skin colour of others, but only at the colour of their souls."

Going more deeply into the spiritual meaning of the painting, he stated that all races exist under one cross. That they all as one are carrying the cross of life. That the cross had been sacred in many religions, and is a universal symbol, no matter how it has been used or misused in the past.

"The Cross," I remember him saying, "is the most powerful symbol which gives you a lot of strength. It symbolizes faith. If you show a cross to the most evil one, he will back away in fear. Evil is opposed to this symbol and does not want people to have faith and strength. But I am not talking about religion. I am talking about God and his higher forces, where all things come from – your inner knowledge, your inner self, your inner inspiration. There is a strength within you that you must bring out, that eases you through all your battles. The Cross is just a part of that, like the saints, angels and archangels." And then he added mysteriously, "It is something that costs you nothing and gives you everything."

Jimi also came up with an idea for a different "Cross Painting", which I later carried out. He wanted me to paint a black woman and a white woman lying over each other in the shape of a cross, the background to be done in the same way as the picture of the four races, only this time in blue. Again, this painting was to show that all races, as well as individuals, are dependent on each other, only jointly constituting a unity. It was also to symbolize that women are equal to men in the eyes of God, as both are His children. He wanted me to do two more paintings, which we discussed afterwards.

Jimi's original plan was for me to start painting the picture while he flew to New York to get his tapes from the Electric Lady Studio, and out of the grip of his manager, Mike Jeffery.

It was the first picture I did after Jimi's death. It helped me to get through a very difficult period of my life: I felt his presence strongly while working on it and I think he helped me to fulfil my task.

"I don't look at things in terms of races. I look at things in terms of people."

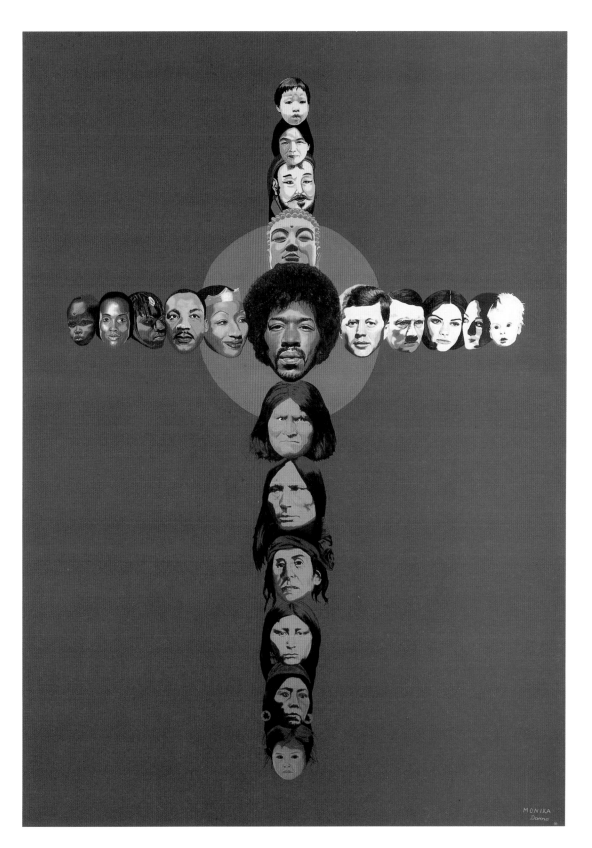

The Last Days

During Jimi's "Cry of Love" tour, which lasted from April to early August 1970 and took him all over America, we kept in touch by letter and phone.

One day he called me, his voice full of excitement. It was now definite, he said, that he would soon be coming to Europe, because his manager had booked a European tour, including a concert at the Isle of Wight Festival at the end of August. He asked me to go to London and rent a flat for us. I was happy and thrilled, for we had been apart for such a long time. I made the arrangements, drove to London, and moved into our flat.

It was a really charming place: the basement apartment of the Samarkand Hotel at 22 Lansdowne Crescent, Notting Hill. This was not a hotel in the usual sense, but rather a house of apartments for rent. Our flat had its own entrance, and in the bedroom were big french windows giving on to a completely secluded little walled garden, surrounded by large shrubs. Behind one of the shrubs was a door leading on to a private garden. Although it was in the heart of London, the flat would give Jimi complete seclusion.

On 27 August Jimi flew in from New York, and late that night we met in the Londonderry Hotel. I remember that it seemed as if we had never been apart, feeling close and at one again immediately. In the hotel lobby Jimi kissed me and whispered in my ear how much he loved me and had missed me, and that he never wanted us to be apart again.

Over the next two days Jimi had to give lots of interviews, and many people he had known in the past wanted to see him. However, we spent as much time together as possible. Jimi loved the flat and wanted it to be kept secret as long as possible so that we could have some privacy. For this reason he retained a hotel room for business meetings, interviews and the like.

Jimi was very happy to be back in England, and was overwhelmed by the affection and interest he was shown. For months his manager, Mike Jeffery, had been telling Jimi that people in Europe had lost interest in him. Jimi now fully realized that this was just another of Jeffery's lies and that, on the contrary, he was still very much appreciated. This encouraged him to mention some of his future ideas in his interviews. The reporters finally also realized that Jimi's image was nothing but a mask.

One such journalist was Roy Hollingworth, who wrote: "Jimi Hendrix, the man with the misleading reputation that had mothers locking away young daughters when he was in town, is talking again... 'It's all turned full circle, I'm back right now to where I started. I've given this era of music everything. I still sound the same, my music's the same and I can't think of anything new to add to it in its present state... Then I started thinking. Thinking about the future. Thinking that this era of music – sparked off by the Beatles – had

Jimi was very happy to be back in England, and was overwhelmed by the affection and interest he was shown.

MONIKA AND JIMI'S FIRST MEETING, JANUARY 1969.

come to an end. Something new has got to come, and Jimi Hendrix will be there. I want a big band. I don't mean three harps and fourteen violins. I mean a big band full of competent musicians that I can conduct and write for. And with the music we will paint pictures of earth and space so that the listener can be taken somewhere!'" Then, at the end of the interview, Jimi said, "I'm happy, it's gonna be good." (*Melody Maker*, 29 August 1970)

What he had said to Roy Hollingworth, I found to be confirmed in reality. Jimi was in a happy mood and full of plans for the future. He invited me to come to the Isle of Wight with him, and on his European tour, which was supposed to last about two weeks. He said he didn't want to be without me, and that in Europe I would be safe from his manager and certain other people.

Jimi also wanted to call his press agent, Les Perrin, to set up a press conference to announce our marriage plans. I felt happy, but at the same time upset, because I was forced to tell Jimi that his plans – both for me to join him on tour, and for him to give the press conference – couldn't be realized. He knew that my father had suffered a bad heart attack and I explained that he was still in a serious condition. His doctors had warned my family that any kind of stress or excitement, good or bad, could trigger another attack, which could be fatal. My mother had been instructed to shield my father from any news that might excite him. Although my father knew that I was with Jimi, to find that we were going to marry – possibly by reading it in the headlines of some newspaper – would certainly have distressed him. It might even have caused another heart attack and his death, and I couldn't build my future happiness with Jimi with that on my conscience.

I had the impression that Jimi agreed with me,

but later that evening, when he mentioned some interviews he had given that day, he told me that one of the reporters had asked him about marriage, and what he had answered. Later on I myself saw the article, which said: "'Marriage is a bit risky now,' he confided, as if hinting at some veiled reasoning. 'I'd really hate to get hurt. That would completely blow my mind.'" (Interview with Mike Ledgerwood, *Disc and Music Echo*, 29 August 1970) Later in the interview Jimi confirmed that he would like to settle down.

I asked Jimi why he was worried about getting hurt. He explained that because I didn't want to commit myself publicly, he was afraid that I did not love him as much as he loved me. I assured him that I loved him more than my life, and that I wanted to announce our love as much as he did, but that we had to wait until my father's health had improved enough for it to be safe.

My father liked Jimi, but feared that we would have a lot of problems from prejudiced people. He believed that if we had children they would suffer through being of mixed race – the world outside, as he put it, being a cruel one. That was the reason for my father's reservations about Jimi and me being together, and I knew that it would agitate and upset my father badly if he found out our plans. I was terrified at the thought that something might happen to him if the news were given out or leaked to the press. Jimi had to promise me not to mention our plans to anyone until the time was right. He expressed his happiness that we both wanted the same thing, and made me promise to let

him know the moment it was safe to announce our love for each other.

To my surprise, Jimi asked if I would have his baby. I knew he loved children, but now he explained that he wanted us to start a family soon. When he came back from his tour ten days later, he told me that if we had a son he would like to call him Wasami. I asked him where he had found this name, and he explained that it was North American Indian, and meant Thunder.

We then talked about Jimi's plans for the future. One of them was to expand the three-piece concept into a bigger band. He was hoping to release his next album in England in October. Since the release of the *Electric Ladyland* double album in autumn 1968, Jimi had not been able to bring out any new albums. (The album *Band of Gypsys*, released in April 1970, had been culled from concert appearances, and formed part of a legal settlement to Ed Chalpin, a manager who had put Jimi under contract in 1965.)

Jimi explained that he had recorded enough music for at least seven or eight albums, but that his manager had prevented him releasing anything, saying the recordings were not commercial enough. In the spring of 1969 Jimi had already announced that he would release a new album that summer, to be called *First Rays Of The New Rising Sun*, but it didn't happen. Months later, in the winter of that year, Jimi announced publicly that he was going to put out a new LP, with the title of either *Shine On Earth, Shine On* or *Gypsy Sun*. He hoped that this would push his manager into

> My father liked Jimi, but feared that we would have a lot of problems from prejudiced people.

releasing an album, but once again Jeffery blocked it. Jimi said how difficult it had been on his last tour to play any new, unreleased material, as it was hard for his fans to relate to songs they had not heard before.

Later on, Jimi told me that there was one thing that really worried him, and that was leaving me alone in London without any protection. Before he had left America for London, Jimi had already mentioned his plans to marry me to some people he trusted, including his father in Seattle and his old friend Mike Quashie in New York. Jimi was afraid that certain people he knew from New York, including his manager, would come to London and might try to harm me once they had found out about our plans. Jimi made me realize, and Billy Cox underlined this, that some people didn't want Jimi to get too close to anyone, as this would give him extra strength to fight and rebel against them. In New York, Jeffery had unsuccessfully tried to bribe Juma Sultan, Jimi's percussionist, to leave him, and other people had been threatened.

Jimi also reminded me of what they had done to him in New York, including the kidnapping, and told me not to forget that they were capable of anything, although he believed I would be much safer in London than in New York. I promised Jimi I would be careful, and he reminded me to watch out for anyone trying to spike my drinks. He also asked me to keep away from certain people and said he would try to call me every day to check I was all right. He added that I should stay in contact with him as much as possible.

When Jimi left for the Isle of Wight Festival we were both unhappy to part again so soon, but knowing it would only be for a short time made it a little easier. Before he left, he wrote a poem which begins:

Sun goddess weeping, never mind
I'll be coming back another time
Where I see those sleepy eyes
Love, natural love I empathize

Mighty Eagles flying high, Knowledge of
    eternal light

Souls will murmur, the Midnight hour
Into her dreams my Love will go
Mighty winds beating high
Expressing all my fearless Emotions

Mighty eagles flying high, knowledge of
    eternal light

Love me always my affinity
Through heavy storms and difficulties.
Powerful spell upon my words...

While playing at the Isle of Wight Festival, Jimi improvised the following lines in "Hey Babe":

Coming back to England,
Thank you baby, for making it so easy
Going through changes in New York, Chicago
Thank you baby for staying here and with me.

These lines had a double meaning, as Jimi pointed out to me later.

While he was on this tour I stayed in our flat, sometimes going to the cinema, or meeting people I knew. During the tour, the last time I spoke to Jimi on the phone was when he was in Berlin, just before leaving to play at the city's Deutschlandhalle

on 4 September. He was in a good mood and looking forward to playing. His next concert appearance – and what would prove to be his final one – was at the Love and Peace Festival on the German Baltic island of Fehmarn on 6 September.

For some days before this concert, Billy Cox, Jimi's bass player, had not been feeling too good, but after the gig he could not continue. Even Jimi wasn't sure what had caused the collapse. However, the remaining concerts of the tour had to be cancelled, and on 7 September the group flew back to London. Jimi did not immediately phone me on his return, and soon I began to realize why.

In the early hours of 8 September, to my surprise, I met Billy Cox at the Speakeasy. Eric Barrett, Jimi's road manager, asked if I could take care of Billy, who was in a very depressed state. Billy told me that he loved Jimi, but could not take it any more, seeing certain "evil" people using, hurting and trying to manipulate him. He was truly upset. He pointed out that whenever he got too close to Jimi, there were others who tried to drive a wedge between them, and that he had run out of strength to oppose these people. Having seen the condition Billy was in, I began to worry about Jimi when I didn't hear from him the next day. I called the Cumberland Hotel, where his management had booked two rooms for him. Jimi had given instructions that he was not to be disturbed, so I left a message asking him to meet me at the Speakeasy that evening.

When we were back at our flat Jimi explained what had happened to Billy, and I could feel how upset it still made him. However, he told me that he was even more worried to think that if Billy had broken down under all the pressure, how could I survive the stress, intrigue and manipulation with which Jimi had to contend all the time?

This thought depressed him and reminded him of the dream he had told me about, and to which he referred in his song "Look Over Yonder". The last couple of days had worried him that his "dream", which he felt was really a warning, might come true in the near future, and he had needed some time to find an answer to this problem.

(There had also been a prediction from a gypsy woman, who had approached Jimi at a fairground before he became successful. She asked if she could read his palm for free, and he agreed. She told him that he would become famous, and that he would also find a "fair flower". When he asked if this "fair flower" was the one for him, and if he was going to be happy with her, the gypsy said yes. But the woman added that she also saw heavy, dark clouds around the two of them, so that he should never be careless.)

Jimi was now even more convinced that I would never be safe in New York, and reminded me that even before all this had happened, he had made plans for us to live in England. This way we would be sufficiently far away from his manager and other people who might want to harm me, just as they had harmed Billy.

He asked me if his love would give me enough strength to take all the pressure once the whole world and not just a handful of people knew about us. I truly loved him and told him that I believed I could take on the world with him by my side.

Being interested in all aspects of this world and the next, Jimi was also fully aware of spiritual powers, whether good or evil, negative or positive. In "Have You Ever Been (To Electric Ladyland)" he said: "Good and Evil lay side by side, while electric Love penetrates the sky." He warned me that alongside mighty positive powers there also exist very strong evil forces, which are constantly striving to sway and control our minds and bodies, and which have exerted an influence over our planet for centuries. Jimi felt that our world is in such confusion because so many people are giving in to these evil powers. All suffering, violence and war, he believed, spring from the influence of such forces, which flourish and find pleasure in the pain they inflict on us and we inflict on ourselves and each other.

When I asked Jimi what could be done to change the situation, he said that it certainly would be no use to sit around just hoping for the best, or simply to go out on the streets and protest. It was up to us all, he believed, to stand up and fight Evil in our minds, our everyday life, and on behalf of the world and the environment.

Every time the subject came up, Jimi spoke most fervently, showing me how strongly he felt and how important he believed it was for the world to shake off this devastating bondage. He said that he had met a lot of people in his life who were not prepared to face reality, preferring to get stoned and remain passive. In his view, even protesting was not enough, without trying to reach the core of the problem and then striving for change.

> Good and Evil lay side by side, while electric Love penetrates the sky.

This lethargy, he believed, was exactly what Evil wanted us to do. The ideal subject for Evil is the person who passively accepts whatever is thrown at him, taking the existing condition of the world for granted. To Jimi, passivity also meant complicity in the unfortunate state of our world.

Jimi warned me that Evil is very clever and adept at fooling people, making them believe in lies, and turning facts upside down. A central lie concerns materialism. People are deliberately guided to worship this scourge, Evil being the ruler of materialism. The more people believe in the power of money, the stronger the hold of Evil on mankind will become. This is one of the traps the evil forces set with great skill. Materialism, according to Jimi, blocks the spiritual awakening and evolution which Evil fears most. Because of the power of money in the world, nothing of genuine value seems to count any more, as everyone is blinded by the desire to gain more and more wealth.

People are running after illusions, unaware that worldly goods are of no eternal value whatsoever. They are just poor artificial substitutes with no authentic or natural qualities – and to Jimi this accounted for the frustration and depression of so many people. It is easy to lose one's way if one forgets the important things in life, such as love, faith and friendship; in other words, all the things that money can't buy.

Jimi also explained to me that Evil uses especially subtle methods to manipulate people's minds, and that the only way to combat these is to constantly reject any negative thoughts that may enter our minds.

Burn everything that represent
the lost ...
destroy the tobacco fields
where chemicals are born to
kill your last breath in your
chest.
Smash all the liquor house
where the devil toasts to
your death ...

demanding any creative input. He felt that children especially were endangered by this flood of shallowness and violence, this pressure for consumption. In some of the commercials he criticized, harmful products such as cigarettes or alcohol were presented as if they could give us a certain social status as well as unlimited pleasure, making us new, happy people, sophisticated in the ways of the world. What these products are doing, said Jimi, is destroying one's mind and body.

Another means of keeping the world from recovery and development is to brainwash people: for example, by promoting the concept that corruption, wars and injustice are a natural and integral part of human nature, and therefore to be condoned. Evil is a master of lies and of disguise, so we should not wait for answers from outside, but should examine ourselves and do everything in our power to see through the veil, and unmask and fight Evil whenever it crosses our path. Only by jointly combatting these forces, Jimi believed, might we be able to bring to a halt the destruction of ourselves, of our children's future, and of the world in general. In fact, it is a fight for the survival of our souls.

In one version of "Look Over Yonder" Jimi wrote:

"The thing is, you have to be positive, you have to keep going until you have all the negatives out of your system." (Interview with Bob Dawbarn, *Melody Maker*, March 1968)

However, according to Jimi, it is not only on earth that there are good and evil planes, but also in the Spiritworld, where some places are like paradise and others like hell. It all depends on one's own spirit and one's past actions as to where one will go. It is our decision which road to take, that of Good or Evil, saved or lost.

The cosmic laws are simple and always just, and by them we will be judged, whether for our actions, or for our passivity if that allows bad things to occur.

Jimi believed that Evil is not only trying but is also succeeding in infiltrating the human mind. One of the most subtle ways is through the media. Jimi was very critical of TV and the dangers it can bring, making people more and more dependent on secondhand information, consumed without

Here comes some news
Coming down like lightning.
Straight from me to you.
People of destruction, your time is out of date.
People who's crooked, better start getting straight.

The next couple of days, Jimi shuttled between our flat and the Cumberland Hotel, meeting various people whom he hadn't seen for a long time. On Tuesday 15 September he decided that he wanted more privacy so that we could spend all of the time together on our own. We stayed mainly in the flat, although Jimi kept his hotel room as a decoy and for incoming messages. There were a few people, including his manager, his lawyer and some others, whom Jimi wanted to avoid for the time being. Only Mitch Mitchell and Chas Chandler knew where he was staying.

From Tuesday until his death we were together every moment, except for two occasions: once when Jimi went backstage for a few minutes at Ronnie Scott's Club, and then on Thursday night, when I left him at a flat for less than an hour. That Tuesday evening Jimi had an appointment with Ed Chalpin, but decided not to go. Later on in the evening we went to Ronnie Scott's for about an hour. We had a table on our own and only the owner of the club joined us for a while. Jimi left for a moment to speak to Eric Burdon and his group, War, backstage. We left the club before they started playing.

We spent these days mostly talking and discussing future plans for ourselves, but also for Jimi's group, music, ideas and so on. He spoke a lot about his spiritual experiences and the knowledge he wanted to share with me, and the messages he wanted to convey through his songs.

Jimi was determined to sort out all his business problems, whatever the cost. These had been immense and had often threatened to suffocate him, but he was feeling strong and positive. Chas Chandler got it right when he said: "It's true to say there are pressures on all musicians, but there were a million on Hendrix."

Jimi discussed with me in detail how he intended getting rid of his manager. Not only had he been told that he had lost his followers in England, but his attempts to come back to this country had been blocked. Jimi believed that Jeffery was afraid that once Jimi was out of his clutches, he would break out of the cage Jeffery had carefully built around him with his promises, lies and threats.

And Jeffery was right. Jimi had also mentioned this problem in an interview on 29 August with Bob Partridge for *Record Mirror*. When asked why the Experience had taken almost two years to return to Britain, Jimi explained: "Even with the Experience, we would be playing in the States and we'd mention that we'd like to come back to Britain to play. But our business people used to tell us 'You're nothing over there in Britain at the moment, besides you've got this booking in Boston on the only date you could make it.' So we never managed to play in Britain after we made it in the States. The business people didn't want us to break out."

On Wednesday 16 September we stayed in our flat the whole day, just talking and feeling happy being together. Jimi spoke of how he wanted to settle down and study music, learn to write music,

> "It's true to say there are pressures on all musicians, but there were a million on Hendrix."

and find a new style, which he had been working on for the past year under the "Sky Church Music" and Band Of Gypsys projects.

Jimi was very serious about the need to learn more about music, and to be able to read music. He said there were so many ideas in his head which he was unable to produce because he had never studied music in a classical sense. He wanted to play a free-form, a purely positive, kind of rock, but using all the elements of music from the past, including classical music, and working it into a completely new style of music.

Already in June 1969, Jimi had said to Nancy Carter: "I like to get into more symphonic things. So then the kids can respect the old music, the traditional, you know, like classics. I like to mix that in with, you know, with the so-called rock today."

He also felt it was important to bring past and present music together. Equally vital, he believed, was to create more understanding and communication between the generations. In his eyes, the so-called "age difference" in years did not exist. He felt it was of no importance how old in years someone is, but rather, as he put it, "how many miles his mind has travelled". A young person can be "old" in those terms, whereas a middle-aged or old person may very well still be a child in respect of their thinking. For Jimi, as long as a person kept his or her mind active and creative, he or she remained young. Only those people whose minds have begun to stagnate can truly be described as old.

Jimi told me that a beginning in trying to close the so-called generation gap was his song "Straight Ahead", in which he tried to convey the necessity of communication between young and old:

Hello my friend

So happy to see you again

I was so alone

All by myself

I just couldn't make it.

Have you heard baby

What the winds blowin' 'round

Have you heard baby

Whole lotta peoples commin' right on down

Communication, yeah, is commin' on strong

I don't give a damn baby

If your hair is short or long

I said get outta your grave

Everybody is dancin' in the street

Do what you know, don't be slow

You gotta practice what they preach

Cause it's time for you and me

Come to face reality

Forget about the past baby

Things ain't what they used to be

Keep on Straight Ahead

Keep on Straight Ahead

Straight up ahead baby

Straight up ahead baby

We got to stand side by side

We got to stand together and organize

Sayin' power to the people

That's what they're screamin'

Freedom of the soul

Pass it on. Pass it on to the young and old

You got to tell the children the truth

They don't need a whole lot of lies

POSTCARD SENT TO MONIKA'S BROTHER BY JIMI THE DAY BEFORE HE DIED.

Because one of these days baby

They'll be runnin' things

So when you give 'em love

You better give it right

Woman and child, man and wife

The best love to have

Is love of life.

Push on ahead baby

Straight on ahead baby.

Hello my friend

So good to see you again

I've been all by myself

I don't think I can make it alone.

Lord, gotta keep on pushin' ahead…

Jimi liked Richard Strauss, Wagner and Beethoven and thought of using music like theirs as a background, combining it with blues and rock – a positive, happy rock. He knew how it should sound, but it was like a baby, still growing inside him, not quite ready to be born. However, he felt he only needed a creative rest in order to give birth to an innovative kind of music. His aim was to create music with healing power, to cure the soul of man and earth.

In his last few weeks Jimi explained to me in more detail the powers which he believed were in everything, including words, numbers and names. He believed that there are deep mysteries hidden in some ancient words.

He said that when positive is reversed it becomes negative. To demonstrate this, he fetched a writing pad and wrote down the word "God", explaining that reversing the letters of this word spells "Dog". While writing, he said that since he had discovered this, he had tried to avoid the use of the word "God".

In the middle of the page he then wrote "Devil", and added the inversion of it underneath, which was "lived". I then knew what he meant. Next he wrote the number 8, explaining that it is often used for evil purposes, and wrote the number 15 in front of the word "Devil", and the sign "=" – 15 equals the Devil. He told me that the opposite applies to the number 7, which is a very special and positive number. He said that the number 7 is full of mysteries. It is the most important number, with many hidden and important meanings.

The earth and the spirit are linked strongly with the number 7. Also, every seventh year, there is a change in the body. It's a circle to put things right, and because of this, everything alters and evolves around it. Jimi pointed out to me that in the past other civilizations had to go through these circles connected with the number 7, going through a peak, and then some sacrifices have to be made, some effort gone through, which he symbolized by drawing a cross over each circle.

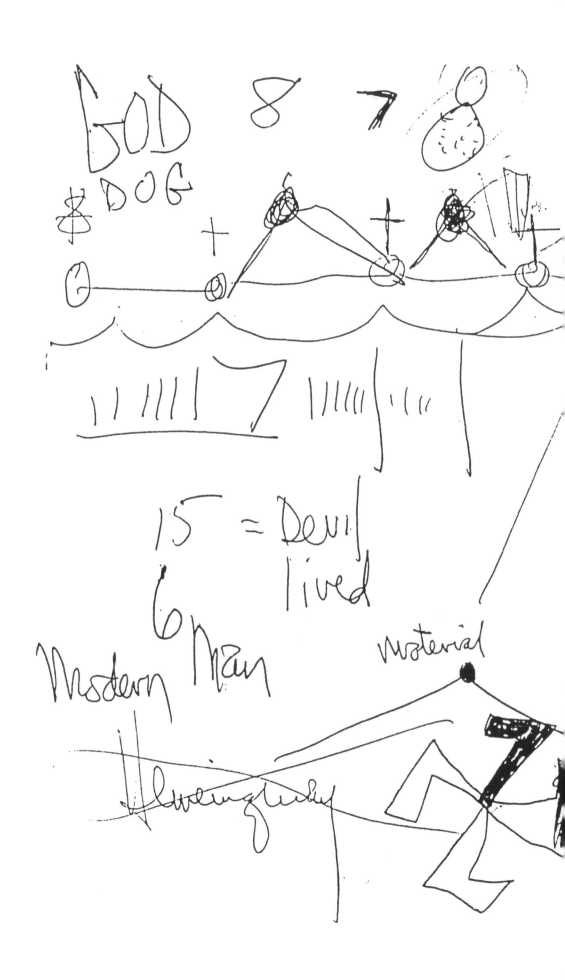

"That is the way evolution happens," he said.

Then Jimi drew four 7s opposing one another, thus forming a spiral of 7s, a symbol which is known as the swastika cross. He explained that it is of vital importance which direction the 7s are pointing in, because this shows whether the symbol has a good or an evil meaning.

On the same sheet of paper he wrote down the words **"Modern Man"** and then, to their right, after a space, **"material"**. The meaning of this is obvious. Above, he wrote the number 6, without seeming to notice it. I mentioned that in Germany it is very impolite to present to somebody a bunch of flowers with an even number. He said thoughtfully that there are a lot of customs that people still practise without knowing the reason, because much knowledge has been forgotten through the ages.

Jimi also mentioned the writer Hemingway and wrote down his name, but unfortunately I can't remember what he said about him.

Later we discussed the meaning and power he believed each person's name carries, and he went into details about our names in particular.

On the afternoon of Wednesday 16 September, Jimi phoned my mother to find out if my father's condition had improved. She said that he was a bit better, and asked Jimi to wait for another two or three days, so that she could break the news gently to him. Jimi was becoming impatient, but agreed to wait, and said he would call her again the next day.

Later on, we drove to Elvaston Place, where a birthday party was being held for Judy Wong, a friend of mine. Many people were there, and while I was talking to some of them Jimi broke his promise and told Judy that he was going to marry me. I only found about this years later when I met Judy again.

From there we drove to Ronnie Scott's. When we entered the club, all the tables were occupied. Jimi pointed out some people he knew from New York who were sitting at a big table. He asked if we should join them and I agreed. A little later he asked me if I would be all right on my own for a while – which was typical of Jimi, always concerned and making sure I was feeling good. He then jammed a few songs with Eric Burdon and War. Soon after we left and drove home.

We talked about various subjects for the next few hours. Then suddenly Jimi started to talk about death. He asked me if, when he died, I would check him over a period of three days to make sure that he was really dead. I asked him why, and he explained that sometimes when a person is on astral travel, his body functions can slow down to such a degree that he is taken for dead. Some people, he said, were just pronounced dead and then buried alive. I agreed to do him this service if need be, because it seemed so important to him. He also mentioned that a few times already in his life he had come near death. One of these instances was when he had a car accident in California. When the time had come for him to die, he said, he would know.

Only ten days before, at the age of twenty-seven, he had told a Danish newspaper: "I'm not sure I will live to be twenty-eight years old." (Interview with Aune Bjørndal, *Morgenposten*, 6 September 1970) I didn't know about this at the time, and he didn't mention it to me. If I had known, I wouldn't have let him out of my sight for

We discussed the meaning and power he believed each person's name carries, and he went into details about our names in particular.

a split second.

We also talked in some depth about the fight between Good and Evil over the destiny of mankind. He told me about the mission for which he believed he had been sent to earth, and which he felt he had not yet completed. One of Jimi's goals, which he had started to work towards and wanted to pursue in the future, was to slowly gather up more and more followers. He wanted to wake people up and make them see what was really going on in the world, showing them directions and solutions for improving the world's situation. He was planning a spiritual movement, gathering as many like-minded people as possible, including other musicians who felt the same way as him and who were willing to spread the word and fight for the cause. He hoped that Bob Dylan would be one of them.

However, Jimi knew that he would first have to convince people that his public image was false, and that it could be a year or two before he would be taken seriously enough to really start establishing his mission. He was willing to sacrifice a great deal and keep on working at it, if people would be willing to take part and listen to what he had to say.

He repeated that he wanted music to be transformed towards something completely new, pure and spiritual, which he also mentioned in one of his last interviews: "In the old civilisations, they didn't have diseases as we know them. It would be incredible if you could produce music so perfect that it would filter through you like rays and ultimately cure!" (Interview with Bob Partridge, *Record Mirror*, September 1970)

Jimi then asked me if I was prepared to help him to spread his message. I agreed, because I felt so strongly about it. He also asked me to promise

him to carry on if he was unable to fulfil his mission. I hesitated, thinking that it would be a mammoth task to tackle on my own, but the way he urged me, I had to give my promise to do so.

In this context he told me that the "Burning Of The Midnight Lamp" in the song of this title symbolized his mission, and that he had also expressed in this song his call for others to join him in his quest.

He also mentioned a new song he had recorded, entitled "Angel", and we got into a conversation about his beliefs and the knowledge he had about angels and archangels. He also expressed his conviction that if Jesus had not died as early as he had, he would have been able to impart twice as much of his message. Jimi thought that much of the true story of Jesus had been lost – for instance, that Jesus had loved Mary Magdalene. The truth about her, according to Jimi, had been partly forgotten, as only a few people around Jesus knew about their spiritual love, and most of them didn't dare to tell the truth. Jimi explained that even though women were looked upon as second-class citizens in those days, after Jesus's death Mary Magdalene claimed his name and carried on his message. He said that the importance of Jesus's woman had been further diminished by the Vatican, hundreds of years ago.

Jimi was genuinely convinced that many of the stories and sayings of Jesus had been lost or manipulated. He believed that Jesus indeed came to earth to convey God's message to mankind, and was sure that Jesus never really died, but that only his earthly body did, while his spirit – an incredibly powerful spirit which was able to materialize physically – lived on. Jimi mentioned Jesus and the Creator quite a few times. At this point I must make it clear that, although Jimi often spoke about

Jesus, he certainly never imagined that he was Jesus, or anyone like him.

At about 7 a.m. we finally fell asleep.

It was just after midday on Thursday 17 September when we woke up. Jimi put on a purple T-shirt of mine, my belt and my green jade necklace, the one I'd been wearing when we first met. He always liked having on something which belonged to me. He also wore his favourite headband, which he had been wearing over the past few months, this time using it as a scarf.

I prepared a little breakfast and, as it was a warm, sunny day, we took it out into the garden. We were both in high spirits, talking and laughing, and again Jimi spoke of his plans for the future. He fetched a writing pad and sketched his idea for a painting he wanted me to do for the cover of his next double album, which he had wanted to call either *Gypsy's Rainbow* or *Rock Of Ages*, but had decided on the latter.

He wanted me to start painting it when he was in New York. His plan was to fly there the following Monday to pick up as many of his tape-recordings of his music as possible, to avoid leaving them in Jeffery's hands. He looked at some paintings I had done and we discussed other ideas for paintings he wanted me to do. He even talked about an art exhibition he hoped to organize for me. I tried to tell him that I was not ready for this, but he didn't accept it.

Jimi made plans to spread his message through his music, and wanted me to help him in this by means of my paintings. The combination of our two arts, he felt, would give more impact to his cause.

He then asked me to take some photographs of him. He had decided to take complete control of his business affairs in regard to his image, which he felt had to be exposed for what it was: something

Jeffery had fabricated for commercial reasons and with which Jimi was still labelled.

He intended to gain control over any pictures, posters and album covers that were published, so that he could give an honest and true picture of the real Jimi Hendrix. The reason why he asked me to help him was, as he said, because I knew him better than anyone else did.

He wanted me to get my camera and take some pictures straight away. I reminded him that it was already late, and we both needed to go to the bank as we had run out of money, but he persuaded me to take some pictures of him first.

When I came back out with the camera, Jimi smiled and walked to the end of the little garden. With a nod of his head, he invited me to follow him. He opened the door leading to the private garden. Someone had left a garden basket full of weeds on the path, and Jimi picked it up. He began to walk towards me, not realizing that I was already taking pictures. It must have been a long time – probably since the days of his youth in Seattle – since Jimi had held a garden basket. Seeing him coming strolling down the path with it, I couldn't help laughing, and he smiled back at me. When he came close he stopped and looked right into the

"The beautiful things are still the same – the sunset and the dew on the grass. No material wealth changes the way I feel about these things."

NEW MUSICAL EXPRESS, SEPTEMBER 1967

camera as I took another shot. He then pretended to pick some fruit from a nearby bush. This was one of the nicest shots of the series. He asked me to take some portraits of him which could be used for paintings. In all of these he was dazzled by the

"I've always loved painting. In fact it was my first love when I was a child."

INTERVIEW WITH BOB PARTRIDGE 1970

sunlight shining directly in his eyes, and I only
noticed this when I saw the pictures later.

　　After this series, Jimi fetched his favourite
guitar, "Black Beauty", and I took some more shots.
We then went back into our own little garden,
where Jimi put his favourite guitar on a chair before

going into the flat. He came out again carrying a teapot, sugar bowl and cups, and placed them carefully on the table. He put a flower, which he had picked earlier in the other garden, into the spout of the teapot. He then went back inside, and this time returned with my favourite peacock-feather choker, which he wound around his guitar. When I asked him why he was doing this, he smiled and said that placing it around his guitar meant bringing together the two most important

"You've got to have love in your heart and try and spread it around."

MELODY MAKER, JANUARY 1969

things in his life – his music and me. Feeling happy and honoured, I went on shooting pictures. Jimi was in a great mood and I had to smile several times while taking the photos. He then asked me to take his place sitting at the table as he wanted to see what it looked like. Before I realized what was going on, he had taken two shots of me. At that time I was shy about anyone taking my picture, and Jimi was aware of it. However, this time he had tricked me, and he laughed because he had caught me by surprise. I jumped up, protesting that it was supposed to be me taking pictures of him, but I had to laugh as well.

The last photograph I took of Jimi was as he was standing in front of the door to our flat. He wanted me to take some more outside, but I had

He told me that he felt he belonged to every race, but that he had found that none of the races really accepted him.

finished the film. Altogether I had taken twenty-six pictures of Jimi, and he had taken two of me.

I quickly drove Jimi to his bank near Marble Arch. As it was impossible to find a parking place, I waited in the car. On returning he asked if I would like to go shopping with him, and we drove to Kensington Market.

We parked in a side road off Kensington High Street. While we walked hand in hand down the High Street, Jimi suggested we should go into Hyde Park and ask someone to take pictures of us together in the park. But I felt too embarrassed, as we would have been surrounded by onlookers, and I persuaded him to have these pictures taken another day in a more private place.

When we reached Kensington Market Jimi bought some clothes, and then we drove to Chelsea Antiques Market in the King's Road. There he spotted some trousers and asked me if I liked them. I said he should try them on. When he came out of the cubicle he looked in the mirror and then came over to me, asking in a whisper whether I thought he could wear them or if they were too tight. I had to hold back my laughter. I wondered what some of the press would say, hearing such a question from the "wild man" of pop. I told him they looked fine, and he bought them.

Jimi took a lot of care over his clothes, especially the colours he wore. He told me that he chose the right colours for himself intuitively, making sure that the blend was right. His mood was also reflected by his clothes, but he felt it was especially important to wear clothes that matched one's aura colours, thus enhancing harmony within oneself. Jimi also designed a lot of his clothes himself.

We were driving further along the King's Road in search of a parking space in one of the side-streets, when Jimi spotted Devon Wilson, from New York, with two other women. He had known Devon for some years, and for several months she had received a salary from his management to take care of him. As Jimi said, she was like a sister and a mother to him for a while, until he saw another side of her he didn't like. He had expressed this in his new single, then about to be released, called "Dolly Dagger". I stopped the car and Jimi exchanged a few words with the women. They asked him to go with them, but he refused. Devon told him that they were giving a party that evening and that he should come along.

Back in the car, Jimi told me he would have to have a serious talk with Devon to stop her bothering me. She and her friend had already made some nasty remarks to me when Jimi was on tour, and on the previous night at Ronnie Scott's. He said he would give her an ultimatum either to behave like a friend and accept our relationship, or to stay out of our life.

We stopped briefly at the Chelsea Drugstore and bought a writing pad and a newspaper. Then Jimi asked me to drive to the Cumberland Hotel, where he wanted to make two phone calls to America and pick up any messages.

By now it was the height of the rush hour and the traffic was pretty heavy. As we drove along, Jimi told me that he wanted to speak to Mitch Mitchell the next day about finding a replacement for Billy Cox. He then turned to the subject of race. He told me that he felt he belonged to every race, but that he had found that none of the races really

accepted him. This seemed to make him sad, because to Jimi the colour of one's skin meant nothing. He never really thought in terms of race; to him all that mattered was a person's character – not the colour of his skin.

When we finally reached Marble Arch we got stuck in the traffic. Waiting for the cars to move again, I saw three young people in another car, waving and laughing at us, and Jimi waved back. They were trying to talk to Jimi across a row of cars, inviting us to come to their flat for a drink. Jimi asked me if we should and I said yes, if he wanted to. They followed us until we parked opposite the Cumberland, and Jimi told them to wait. As we were walking to the hotel, I asked Jimi where he knew them from. He looked at me in surprise, saying he thought they were my friends. We both laughed.

Jimi had made up his mind that he was definitely going to break up with his manager. It was a difficult decision for him, especially as he knew that a lot of his unreleased music could fall into Mike Jeffery's hands, which was exactly what he feared the most – that someone else would meddle with his music. So this decision was a real sacrifice for Jimi, as he was sure that Jeffery would alter some of his music to make it more commercial and marketable. However, having gone through such a long and difficult period with his manager – he had suffered threats, blocking of his new albums, and the creation of a false image through being told

Jimi had made up his mind that he was definitely going to break up with his manager.

what to do and how to appear in public – Jimi felt this was the only way out of a disastrous situation. He wanted to destroy his fabricated image and produce new music, whereas Jeffery thought the opposite and wanted to keep everything exactly as it was. A split with Jeffery would also mean that Jimi and I would have a chance to live together without fear.

Jimi picked up the telephone and asked me to listen carefully to what he had to say to his lawyer, Henry Steingarten. He came straight to the point, telling his lawyer that he wanted to leave Jeffery for good, no matter what the cost might be. Steingarten, who was in partnership with Jeffery's lawyer, asked Jimi if he had thought about the consequences, without making clear exactly what he meant by this. Jimi answered firmly that he had, and told his lawyer to proceed with his instructions.

Jimi then called the Electric Lady Studios in New York and left a message for Eddie Kramer, his engineer, that he would be flying in on Monday. A short while later we left the hotel, and as we passed through the lobby I reminded Jimi to pick up his messages, but he said they could wait another day.

The three young people were still waiting outside and we followed them in the car to their flat, where we stayed for about an hour. It was around 8.15 in the evening when we arrived home. I parked the car and walked towards the flat. Looking back, I saw Jimi doing something to the car's rear window. I walked back to him, wondering what was wrong, and saw that he had written "I Love You" on the dusty window with his fingertip.

Back in the flat the phone was ringing, but before I could pick it up Jimi told me to say that he wasn't in. It was Mitch Mitchell, wanting to talk to Jimi. Just as I was saying he wasn't there, Jimi started pulling the most hilarious faces, trying to

make me laugh. I barely made it through the conversation with Mitch without bursting into laughter. When I'd hung up I told Jimi that it was unfair to do that when I was making excuses for him, but he just smiled and said he would talk to Mitch a bit later. A few minutes later Chas Chandler called, and again I had to make the same excuse while Jimi pulled all kinds of faces. Afterwards we just couldn't stop laughing. Jimi said he would speak to Chas later, too. He wanted Mitch and Chas to visit us the next day to discuss choosing a new bass player and other business matters.

Jimi then rang my mother again to see how my father was, and she promised to break the news to him in the next day or two.

I cooked a meal for us while Jimi had a bath and washed his hair. He came dressed all in purple and mauve, with my mauve belt around his waist. We had a bottle of white wine with our meal, Jimi drinking more of it than me. He helped with the washing up and then we sat in the living room.

I asked Jimi to describe some more of the meanings and stories behind his songs. I could never have enough of listening to these explanations. Sometimes there were complete stories behind the different movements, as Jimi called them, of one song or lyric. In the earlier songs he frequently used symbols to express himself and one needed to know these to fully understand his lyrics. At the beginning of his career he had felt that he should conceal some of the things he wanted to convey, because the time was not right for him to speak openly.

Later on we talked about our future. Jimi was looking forward so much to us having a baby, and already making plans for it. He intended we should marry in Germany the following month, October

He had written "I Love You" on the dusty window with his fingertip.

"*Wherever I will be, my spirit will always be in you. Never forget what I have just said.*"

intense voice, he said he wanted me to keep this poem for ever. What he had written down, he said, was the story of him and me, and that I should never give it away.

Jimi had given me poems before, but never accompanied by such words. Curious to find out what he had written, I started to read. However, at the first line Jimi distracted me by talking, making me forget about the poem for the time being.

After talking for a while about some of the meanings and powers certain names can generate, suddenly he said, very intensely, "Wherever I will be, my spirit will always be in you. Never forget what I have just said."

I asked Jimi what he meant. He looked directly into my eyes and, very seriously, repeated, "Wherever I will be, my spirit will always be in you." Still I didn't understand, and asked again what he was trying to say. For a moment he was silent, until finally he replied, "I could be touring. I just want you to remember that my spirit will always be in you whether I am personally with you or not." He then kissed me and changed the subject.

Only later, after his death, did I fully understand the meaning of these words.

We continued talking about various spiritual issues, some of which I wanted to know more about. At about 1.45 a.m. Jimi told me that he had put something off all evening which now he felt he must do. He explained that he wanted to go to the party to which Devon had invited him, in order to warn her to leave me alone. Jimi thought that her intention was to cause a rift between him and me. He was worried that while he was in New York she might take the opportunity to harass or even harm me. Also, he warned me again about certain other people. He made me promise that if anything

1970, when he would be touring there. Later, after the tour of Germany and England, he wanted us to get a house outside London, in the countryside.

Then Jimi picked up his guitar and started to play while I washed my hair. When I returned he had stopped and was writing something down. I kept quiet, not wanting to disturb him. I watched him writing – he put it all down at once without hesitation, as if it was flowing out of him.

He then stood up and put the writing pad in my hand. Looking into my eyes, and in a very

Both of us still felt very happy as we talked about our future.

should happen while he was away, I should at once return to my family in Germany, where I would be safe until he came back.

I drove him to the party and he asked me to ring him about half an hour later, as he didn't want to stay long. He first asked me to join him, but we both decided it was better if he went alone. I drove home and phoned him as agreed, but he said he hadn't had a chance to speak to Devon yet, and that I should ring back about ten minutes later. I did so, and he asked me to fetch him at once.

When I arrived at the house, Jimi was just coming out. He said it had been hopeless, because Devon had been too stoned to speak to seriously. He would have to try again the next day.

He opened his hand, showing me various drugs in pill form, and said all these had been given to him at the party. I asked him if he had taken any, but he said he hadn't and threw them down the drain in the street. Some of the people at that party called themselves his friends, but I wondered what sort of friends some of them were to give him all those drugs which could only harm him.

We arrived back at the flat at about 3 a.m. For some time we talked in detail about Faith, and that the power of Faith and the power of Love were the strongest forces in existence. We also had a deep discussion about the Spiritworld and its various dimensions. Jimi described everything so vividly that I was spellbound just listening to him.

At about 4 a.m. Jimi wanted to take a couple of sleeping tablets, because although he didn't feel at all sleepy, he needed to get some rest. We knew that he faced a heavy schedule of meetings from later morning right through the rest of the day. I persuaded him to wait a little longer, hoping he would fall asleep naturally. Jimi said he felt hungry, so I made him a tuna sandwich, but he

only had a bite.

We carried on discussing life after death. I asked Jimi what happens to people who commit suicide. He explained that it depended on the circumstances, but normally the spirit of such a person would by no means be redeemed, as they probably hoped, but would have to go through much more pain than it had ever felt on earth. We spoke on this subject for some time, until Jimi started to talk about reincarnation, and some of the previous lives he could recall.

Even though it was now six o'clock in the morning, I was so fascinated by his knowledge that I felt wide awake. I knew I would probably not get to sleep now, but thinking about Jimi's heavy business meetings in a few hours' time, I secretly took one sleeping tablet in the hope that I might drop off and Jimi would fall asleep too. I wanted to be able to help and support him as best I could the following day, and it would be difficult if I was too exhausted.

This was not a normal practice for me. Although I did have about forty-five prescribed sleeping tablets, in packets of ten, in a large cupboard opposite the bed, they were left over from two operations I had recently undergone in Germany. I had seldom seen Jimi take anything to help him sleep and then only if it was really necessary – that is, when he had something important to do the next day and he couldn't sleep. A few days earlier he had taken one of my tablets, and it had taken him an hour to fall asleep.

Both of us still felt very happy as we talked about our future. Then, to my surprise, Jimi picked up his necklace with the crucifix from the table and put it on. I had never seen him go to sleep wearing his crucifix before. I was still wondering why he had done this, when he started to describe various visions he had had, and explained the meaning of some of the symbols which appeared in them. Jimi was still wide awake and talking animatedly, but, fascinated as I was, it was now 7 a.m. and I was beginning to feel sleepy.

Jimi noticed I was getting tired and asked if he should be quiet. I smiled at him, feeling happy lying in his arms, my head resting on his chest. I said he should keep on talking, but apologized in advance in case I should fall asleep. He smiled and kissed

The last time I looked at the clock it was about 7.10. Soon afterwards I fell asleep in Jimi's arms. It was Friday 18 September.

me, and went on describing more of his visions. The last time I looked at the clock it was about 7.10. Soon afterwards I fell asleep in Jimi's arms. It was Friday 18 September.

Three hours later, at about 10.20, I woke up, feeling exhausted yet at the same time wide awake. I looked at Jimi, who was sleeping normally, his face towards me. I tried to nod off again, realizing how little I had slept, but gave up after about fifteen minutes. I was just too restless, thinking about all the things we, and especially Jimi, had to do that day. I knew that he hadn't had enough sleep yet to be on good form for a busy schedule. I slipped out of bed very gently so as not to wake him, and cautiously tiptoed into the bathroom, had a wash and put on some make-up. On my way to the kitchen I again tiptoed through the bedroom,

I tried immediately to wake him, shaking him and calling his name, but in vain.

seeing that Jimi was still asleep.

I had some breakfast, and then wanted a cigarette, but found that we had run out. I knew Jimi wouldn't like me to go anywhere without telling him, but decided it was more important for him to sleep. I made the decision to pop out and buy some cigarettes. I went back to the bedroom, had a close look, and saw that Jimi was sleeping peacefully. Then I quickly left the flat and walked to the shop, which was just a few doors away. I bought a packet of cigarettes and returned to the flat. This took no more than perhaps ten minutes.

I unlocked the front door quietly and tiptoed softly into the bedroom. In the meantime Jimi had turned over, and was now lying with his face to the right, whereas when I went out he was on his left side.

I went to the side of the bed and sat down on a chair, looking at Jimi, thinking how much I loved him and how happy I was. I lit a cigarette, and suddenly noticed a tiny trickle coming from Jimi's mouth. It was after 11 a.m., but I didn't know exactly what time. It was clear Jimi was being sick. I tried immediately to wake him, shaking him and calling his name, but in vain.

He was still breathing. I stepped on something, and looking down saw a sleeping tablet packet on the floor. Picking it up, I saw all ten tablets were missing. (Later, a policeman found one tablet on the floor, slightly concealed by the edge of the bed.)

I knew I had to get help at once and remembered that Jimi's private doctor was a Dr Robertson. In Germany, in similar circumstances, you call your private doctor first, as he is the one who knows best what to do, being familiar with his patient's history. But when I looked in the telephone directory there were several doctors of the same name listed and I couldn't remember the man's first name or his address.

I then decided to ring an acquaintance of mine, Alvinia Bridges. I knew that Dr Robertson had several musicians as patients (including members of the Beatles), and Alvinia had contacts in the music world. I hoped she would know his number. She wasn't in, but our friend Judy Wong gave me a number where I could reach her.

Alvinia answered the phone, and I told her that Jimi had taken some sleeping tablets and was being sick, and that I couldn't wake him. She didn't know the doctor's number, and suggested I call an ambulance, to which I agreed. Eric Burdon, who was with Alvinia, suddenly came on the phone, saying there was no need to worry and that I should wait and see if Jimi woke up on his own. I said I thought I should call an ambulance at once, and Eric replied, "Then call the fucking ambulance."

I dialled 999 immediately, saying it was an emergency, explaining what had happened and asking them to hurry up.

I dialled 999 immediately, saying it was an emergency, explaining what had happened and asking them to hurry up. Later on I found the call had been logged at 11.18 a.m.

I checked the drawer quickly to make sure Jimi had taken only one packet of tablets, and to my relief saw the three other packets still there. I was not in too much of a panic, because I knew that Jimi could have only taken the tablets within the last three hours, after I had fallen asleep. I had read an article saying that sleeping tablets normally only take their full effect after seven hours. And anyway I was sure that the number he had taken was not a fatal dose.

Alvinia rang back and asked me which hospital Jimi would be taken to. I said I didn't know yet as the ambulance hadn't come, but promised to call her from the hospital on our arrival. While waiting for the ambulance, I again tried to wake Jimi, but without success. His head was still lying on one side. I checked his pulse, which I had learned to do after my father's heart attack, and found it was normal compared with mine, as was his breathing.

I held his hand, sitting by his side and watching him. I simply couldn't imagine that anything serious would ever happen to Jimi. I was still under the spell of all the joy and confidence in the future that we had felt together only a few hours before. For me, being with Jimi had always been like floating in a beautiful dream, and even more so during these recent weeks. He was the love of my life, and I couldn't believe anything could happen to him.

I wondered what Jimi's reaction would be to waking up in hospital. I didn't care whether he was upset with me or not – I had had no option but to call the ambulance. But my hope was that the press wouldn't find out. That is the reason why I didn't mention Jimi's name to the two ambulance men when they arrived.

Countless thoughts had floated through my mind while I had been waiting, time seeming to drag by unbearably slowly, although the ambulance took only nine minutes to come, arriving at 11.27. I explained the situation to the crew. They seemed to feel no need to hurry, behaving quite calmly. While I told one of them what had happened, the other looked into Jimi's eyes and checked his heart and pulse. Having done so, he diagnosed that Jimi was only in a deep sleep because of the sleeping tablets. He said I shouldn't worry at all: Jimi would wake up as soon as the effect of the tablets wore off, but they would take him to hospital anyway, just to be on the safe side.

> I held his hand, sitting by his side and watching him. I simply couldn't imagine that anything serious would ever happen to Jimi.

While one man went out to fetch an ambulance chair, the other told me that they saw plenty of cases like this. He said we would probably be leaving the hospital together that afternoon, laughing about the whole affair. Still worried, I nevertheless felt some relief on hearing this. I believed that Britain's ambulance staff were extensively trained, and I had full trust in what these men were doing.

They lifted Jimi and sat him upright in the ambulance chair, then carried him up the cast-iron spiral staircase to the street. Meanwhile I quickly collected the packet and prescription for the sleeping tablets in order to show the doctor at the hospital what Jimi had taken. They were a German brand called Vesparax.

After the men had lifted Jimi in the chair into the ambulance, I climbed in next to him and the driver set off, with the other man sitting in the back watching Jimi. The driver used the siren only once, when we encountered heavy traffic. Throughout the journey the man in the back made sure that Jimi's head stayed in a slightly backward-titled position. Several times Jimi's head dropped forward on to his chest, but on each occasion the man pushed it back. Months later I was told that the best position would have been to have Jimi lying flat with his head turned to the side.

Again the ambulance man told me not to worry, that everything was going to be all right and that Jimi was only in a deep sleep. The drive seemed to take ages, and I became concerned. Later I found out that the nearest hospital, the one for our district, was quite close to our flat. However, the driver had been radioed that it was completely full and told to go to another hospital which, unfortunately, was much farther away. Just as we passed inside the gates of St Mary Abbots Hospital, off Kensington High Street, I saw the ambulance man getting nervous and putting an oxygen mask over Jimi's face. From then on, everything happened very quickly. The driver stopped in front of the hospital entrance and a doctor and a nurse rushed Jimi inside. Our arrival was later stated to have been at 11.45 a.m.

I tried to follow Jimi, but was stopped by a nurse, who instructed me to sit in the waiting room. I was too restless to sit still, and felt that

> The ambulance man told me not to worry, that everything was going to be all right and that Jimi was only in a deep sleep.

Jimi was behind one of the doors leading into other rooms. I was just about to enter one of them, when a young doctor came out. I begged him to tell me that Jimi was all right. He asked me to explain what had happened. I gave him the tablet packet and prescription and told him what I knew.

I felt a certain attitude coming from him, and at that point I became very nervous, wondering if Jimi was really being taken care of in the best possible way. So I tried to press the doctor into action by telling him that he was dealing with JIMI HENDRIX. This didn't seem to impress him at all, so I explained that Jimi was a very famous musician and composer and that nothing must happen to him. This didn't seem to work either. In desperation I demanded that he should treat Jimi privately and that I would cover the whole cost of the private treatment. "All right," he said, and left. Only later did I find out that this hospital offered no private medical care at all.

The doctor's attitude had made me feel uneasy, and I thought I needed a man to make sure everything possible was done for Jimi. I phoned Alvinia, and asked her to tell Gerry Stickles, Jimi's tour and road manager, to come to the hospital immediately. I became more and more nervous and worried. As I couldn't bear it any longer, I opened the door to the room where I thought Jimi was being treated. Inside I was stopped by a nurse who pushed me back into the waiting room again. But for a few seconds I saw Jimi lying there, being worked on by a doctor and a nurse.

Another nurse ordered me to sit down and keep quiet. I felt completely alone and helpless, praying that Jimi would be all right, as I loved him beyond description. I hoped desperately that Gerry would come soon to take over and make sure that everything possible was done for Jimi.

After a while I couldn't sit still a moment longer, so I went back into the room where Jimi lay, only to be pushed out again. For a second I saw the doctor bending over Jimi. I couldn't make out exactly what he was doing. Again I was told to sit in the waiting room.

I was trying to work out why Jimi had swallowed so many sleeping tablets. The only answer I could find was that after I had fallen asleep he had taken the two tablets he had planned to take earlier. Then, as these wouldn't have worked as fast as Jimi expected, he had taken some more, unaware that his mind was already clouded by the effect of the first two tablets. And yet I was absolutely certain that it was not a suicide attempt, for this

A nurse came over, saying I shouldn't cry because Jimi was all right again.

would have been completely contrary to Jimi's nature and his spiritual beliefs. Indeed, if he had wanted to commit suicide, why hadn't he taken all forty-five tablets in the cupboard?

A few minutes later I felt that something had gone utterly wrong, and I burst out crying. A nurse came over, saying I shouldn't cry because Jimi was all right again. She explained that his heart had stopped, but that they had managed to get it going

again, and Jimi was all right now. Alvinia was with me at that point, and she told me recently that she remembers well how the nurse came up to us and said he was alive and not to worry. For a time the nurse's words gave me comfort and hope. I was wishing and praying with all my heart that nothing serious would happen to Jimi.

Then suddenly I started trembling with fear, sensing something dreadful was going on. It was an awful feeling: I was absolutely terrified. I tried to fight this fear, but it overwhelmed me.

A little later another nurse came up to me, and said, "I'm sorry, but he passed away." I sensed what she meant, but I didn't want to believe her, and asked her to explain. "He is dead," was her reply.

I had lost Jimi, the love of my life. My soul cried out in pain and despair. In a split second my love, my hopes and the purpose of my life had all come to an end. I felt so terribly lonely. It was as if the pain was cutting me into pieces, and I couldn't stop weeping.

I pleaded with the nurse to let me see Jimi one last time. I remembered his request that, if he were pronounced dead, I should make sure it was really so. (Strangely enough, many years later I found out from Jimi's father that when Jimi died a guy called up and said," Why don't you go down to the funeral home and check his body? He might have been in suspended animation, because he had this magic.") However, it was denied to me to watch over Jimi for three days as I had promised him. Because we were not yet married, I had no right to.

The nurse doubted that it would be possible even to see Jimi again, as it was against the rules, but I insisted, telling her I couldn't leave the hospital until I had seen him. She said she would

try to get permission for me and left. I kept crying, as did Alvinia, who was trying to comfort me at the same time. When Gerry Stickles and Eric Barrett

"I'm sorry, but he passed away."

arrived they asked me how Jimi was. With tears running down my face I tried to tell them. On the hospital's death certificate it was later stated that Jimi died at 12.45 p.m.

While I was waiting to see Jimi I felt as if my soul was bleeding. About twenty minutes later a nurse allowed me to go and see him. I was still weeping, but the moment I entered the room and saw Jimi lying on some kind of stretcher I couldn't cry any more. The same thing happened to Alvinia, who had followed me in.

There was something in that place – I can't really describe it. The room was filled with an atmosphere of complete peace. Jimi looked like he was just sleeping, with a faint smile on his face, as if he was having a beautiful dream. For a long time I just looked at him, caressing his face. I felt he was happy. Then I kissed Jimi goodbye.

Only later that day did I read Jimi's last poem, remembering his words when he handed it to me.

For a long time I just looked at him, caressing his face. I felt he was happy. Then I kissed Jimi goodbye.

(slow)

the Story — of Jesus
so easy to explain .
after they crusified him,
a woman, she claimed his
name '
the story — of Jesus .
the whole Bible knows —
went all across the Desert,
and in the middle he found a rose,

there should be no questions
there should be no lies —
He was was married ever
happily after —
for all the tears we cry —
No use in arguing — all
the use to man the means —
when each man falls in Battle, his
soul it has to roam

angels — of heaven
flying saucers to some

"THE STORY OF LIFE", JIMI'S LAST POEM.

made easter Sunday
the name of the Rising
Sun —

the story ... is written
by so many people
~~so many people~~ who dared
to lay down the truth ———
to So ~~so~~ very many who cared
to ~~say~~ carry ~~the~~ cross
of Jesus and beyond ———

We will guild the light
this time with a woman in our
arms ———

We ~~as~~ men —
can't explain the reason why —
the women's always mentioned
at the moment that we die —
All we know ———
is God is by our side

and he says the word

So easy yet so hard —
I wish not to be alone
So I must respect my other
heart

Oh — the story —
of Jesus — is history
Of you and me — No use in
feeling lonely

I am you searching to be free

the story —
of life is quicker
than the wink of an eye

the story of love —
is hello and goodbye
until we meet again

Stairways from Beyond

AFTERWORD

From the hospital, Gerry Stickles, Eric Barrett and Alvinia Bridges took me back to the flat. Gerry told me I had to leave immediately because reporters would come, wanting to find out about Jimi's death.

The police arrived, and in tears I tried to tell them what I knew. They looked around the flat and found the one sleeping tablet under the bed. They didn't ask for any of Jimi's writings, but they looked through some papers, including the last poem that he had given to me. They didn't take anything away with them. I was glad about this later, especially when I found out that most of Jimi's belongings which weren't in our flat had been sent, not to Jimi's father Al Hendrix, but to Mike Jeffery, Jimi's manager, who later sold most of them.

The police warned me not to say a word about what had happened, especially not to the press. After their visit I was taken to a hotel where Eric Burdon and his band were staying. It was the first time I had met him in person. He and Alvinia took care of me for the next three days.

Gerry Stickles and Eric Burdon urged me to hide away somewhere outside London, so that no one could find me and ask questions, but I refused to leave town.

Left in the hotel, I was overwhelmed by

feelings of loneliness and utter despair. The pain of losing Jimi was almost unbearable. I had never realized how much pain one person could feel. It was as if a part of me had died with Jimi. And the feelings were to stay with me for many months, even years. I was in deep shock. Only one thing, which Jimi had said to me the night before he died, would help me through the years. He had told me never to forget that, wherever he was, his spirit would always be in me.

I was still bewildered as to why Jimi had to die after taking only nine sleeping tablets. The coroner and some top doctors I consulted months later in Germany also confirmed that it was not a fatal dose. I remember in the hospital after Jimi's death, a sister said that the doctor had told her that Jimi didn't die from the sleeping tablets, but from something that got stuck in his windpipe. He was still alive when the nurse spoke to me and Alvinia. The German specialists asked me why Jimi had not been given a tracheotomy to allow him to breathe. I couldn't answer, as I didn't understand it myself. Given the way Jimi died, I felt something must have gone terribly wrong, but I couldn't put my finger on what it was.

A man told me to keep quiet about everything concerning Jimi's death or else something nasty could happen to me.

I was again urged by Gerry to leave London, and again I refused. Soon afterwards I received a phone call. A man told me to keep quiet about everything concerning Jimi's death or else something nasty could happen to me. I have no idea who it was or why I got this call, but at that time only a few people knew where I was staying. However, I was too depressed to really care about

the threat.

I learned that Jimi would be buried in his home town of Seattle. This made me very sad, as he had told me that if he died he didn't want to be buried in Seattle, but on the banks of the Thames in London. But unfortunately there was nothing I could do about this.

Later the coroner (or one of his officers) came to ask me the same questions as the police. He told me that the police had checked the flat where Jimi had spent about an hour the night before his death. They had found the flat empty – everyone had disappeared. Before he left, he warned me not to interfere with his investigations by talking to the press before the coroner's inquest.

Eric Burdon and Alvinia told me that Eric's band had a concert in Newcastle the next day and that it would be better for me to come along. I agreed, as I felt too vulnerable to stay on my own. My mother wanted to come over and support me, but I asked her to stay with my father for the next few days until the worst impact of the news had worn off, because I was worried for him.

The next day, Saturday 19 September, we drove to the station to catch the train to Newcastle. From the car to the train, they put a blanket over my head to hide me from the reporters. They had reserved a carriage for the band, and hid me in the toilet until the train left the station. Then I realized, to my surprise, that some reporters were coming with us, taking pictures and filming the band. Eric assured me that they had only come to film him. Even so, I felt very uncomfortable and unhappy.

An hour later I asked if anyone had an aspirin as I had a splitting headache. Someone gave me a tablet. After a while I felt very strange, drifting away and losing touch with reality. I found out later that I had been given LSD or something like it. To this day I am amazed that anyone could give acid to someone with a headache, knowing that person to be in deep shock and unused to taking drugs. I can't remember much of the rest of the journey or our arrival in Newcastle.

I had been told by the police, the coroner and Gerry Stickles to remain silent, but no one had bothered to tell me about the newspaper headlines which appeared worldwide concerning Jimi's death. These reported that he had died of a drug overdose, some even stating that it was an overdose of heroin.

Two days after Jimi's death, one Sunday newspaper published a picture of Kathy Etchingham, a former girlfriend of his, and her husband – she had married in 1969. In the article, allegedly in Kathy's own words, Jimi was described as a violent, hard-drinking, drugged-up sex maniac – a "wild man".

Equally damaging was a headlined story describing Jimi's last days. In the piece, a girl named Lorraine James said that Jimi had attended a sex party in a completely drugged-up state on the night before his death. She said the party had lasted until the early hours of Friday, the day he died. A couple of months later an insurance investigator exposed the story as complete fiction, but this, like so many other things, was never made public.

The day we came back from Newcastle, Monday 21 September, Eric Burdon gave a TV interview in which he stated that he believed Jimi had committed suicide. I was stunned and dismayed, as he knew through me that this was not true. Years later, Eric admitted that he had got stoned before going on screen, and acknowledged that he had said something wrong. In his autobiography *In the Wink of an Eye* he said: "In defiance of everybody and everything and all that

Jimi stood for, I got stoned before the interview… I only care that my ego was stupid enough to allow me to speak publicly about the death of a friend, for my feelings I couldn't put into words, they were scrambled, disconnected, senseless, not words, just feelings pouring out." I realized at the time that Eric felt very close to Jimi and had been badly hurt by his death.

Another story invented by a newspaper, and which was frequently repeated over the years, was the report of the "Help me, man" message that Jimi

Tabloid write-ups kept spreading and repeating rumours and half-truths as facts all over the world.

was alleged to have left on Chas Chandler's answerphone. Chas himself denies ever having received such a message: hardly surprising, considering the fact that in 1970 he had no answerphone at all.

All Jimi's efforts over the previous two years to distance himself from his wild image, trying to make the press and his fans aware of his artistic and spiritual side, were destroyed in the space of a few days. Tabloid write-ups kept spreading and repeating rumours and half-truths as facts all over the world. And they achieved their purpose in making the "wild man" a sex maniac, a drug addict, and, above all, a drug casualty. This fitted in nicely with the best-selling cliché of rock stars becoming victims of their excessive lifestyle.

This utterly false reputation was to stay with Jimi until this day, obscuring the message of Love, Peace, Freedom and Brotherhood that he tried to

spread through his music and which he felt was the purpose of his life.

Worried about this misrepresentation, I asked Gerry Stickles to set up a press conference through Jimi's press agent, Les Perrin. I was desperate to clear Jimi's memory of all the lies being spread about him, and decided to go against the coroner's orders and express myself publicly. Gerry informed me and my brother, Klaus-Peter, who had come to support me, that the press conference could take place at 3 p.m. on the day of the inquest, ten days after Jimi's death.

In the meantime I gave an interview to a reporter from the German magazine *Stern*, but for some mysterious reason it was never published. I also approached various other, mainly English newspapers but only managed to give one interview. The rest of the press were not interested, and some even said they couldn't print a different story of Jimi's death so soon because it would show them up for not having reported the facts correctly the first time. I was forced to accept that it was too late to undo the damage caused by an irresponsible, sensation-seeking press, and my only hope lay with the inquest and the press conference.

At the inquest Gerry Stickles testified that at the time in question Jimi was stable and well, did not appear depressed, and had not been in the habit of using hard drugs.

Professor Donald Teare, one of the country's leading forensic scientists, presented the post-mortem report. He said they had found sleeping tablets – Vesparax – in Jimi's body. Jimi had taken nine of them. The normal dosage specified on the packet was a half to one tablet. Professor Teare said they also found small traces of another barbiturate, Seconal, and 20mg of amphetamine. No hard drugs were found in Jimi's body, nor any needle marks –

the signs of drug addiction which never disappear. He confirmed that the dose of sleeping tablets was too low to be fatal. Only a small amount of alcohol was detected. It was estimated that the alcohol content was just under the drink-driving limit at the time Jimi took the tablets. Only much later did I discover that a compound which could not be

The official cause of death was "inhalation of vomit due to Barbiturate intoxication".

analysed was found in Jimi's body.

At that time it was common in England to carry out the post-mortem several days after a person had died, which meant that certain poisons, for example, would no longer be detectable.

Only Gerry Stickles, the pathologist, a policeman and myself were questioned at the inquest. No one else: neither the people in the flat Jimi had visited that night, nor the ambulance men, nor the hospital doctors, were required to testify. I was stunned. I was a foreigner in England, but I had assumed that if an inquest was held all persons involved would be questioned openly in court, to find out the true circumstances, especially in a case of suspicious death.

In his final statement the coroner simply declared that Jimi had died in hospital and that he had taken a large dose of sleeping tablets but not enough to have been fatal: normally he would have

been expected to recover. The official cause of death was "inhalation of vomit due to Barbiturate intoxication". As there was no evidence as to an intention to commit suicide, the coroner recorded an open verdict, which the jury returned.

For me the inquest had not answered the vital question. If the number of tablets Jimi had taken was not large enough to be fatal, then why did he have to die?

Worse was to come. When I left the inquest I was very upset. I was now pinning all my hopes on the press conference, where I hoped to be able to clear up the lies which had been spread about Jimi over the past ten days. I also wanted to question publicly why Jimi had had to die and to mention some other facts – for example, the situation between Jimi and Mike Jeffery – which I thought were important for everyone to know. Naturally I was nervous about appearing in public, but at the same time I felt strongly that this was the only ray of hope.

An hour before the press conference I received a call from Gerry Stickles, telling me it had been cancelled. I was devastated. My brother tried to comfort me as best he could. I was convinced it was Jeffery who had put a stop to it. It was not in his interests to have the truth exposed.

For me the inquest had nor answered the vital question.

In fact, for a couple of reasons I believe it was convenient for Jeffery to have Jimi labelled a drug addict. One was that in the past few months Jimi had come closer to discovering where huge amounts of his money had disappeared to, and he was in the process of investigating this. If someone had now asked Jeffery where all the money had gone, he would have had a perfect excuse,

answering that Jimi obviously didn't really know what he was talking about, as he must have taken too many drugs.

I was told later that Buddy Miles, one of Jimi's drummers, had a feeling that Jeffery didn't want a big funeral for Jimi, mainly because he feared Miles would go public with what he knew about Jeffery and the missing money.

Most of the papers which had filled their front pages with stories about Jimi dying of a drug overdose, having attended sex parties and so on, did not bother to report the outcome of the inquest, let alone mention that Jimi did not die of a drug

I believe it was convenient for Jeffery to have Jimi labelled a drug addict.

overdose or that no needle marks were found.

It was also strange how so many people suddenly declared they had been Jimi's friends. Some felt a need to say that they had seen Jimi the day before he died. By their accounts, he would have been in two or three different places at the same time.

The day after the inquest Klaus-Peter drove me back to Germany, where I tried to find newspapers that would be interested in printing the true version of events. Also, I later contacted some American papers. However, I met with the same reaction as before. A couple of them seemed to regret what they had printed, and said I should try again in a few months' time: perhaps by then they would be ready for the true story.

I was shattered, and fell into utter despair. Not

Not only had I lost Jimi, but I was completely powerless to remedy the damage which had been inflicted on his reputation and memory.

only had I lost Jimi, but I was completely powerless to remedy the damage which had been inflicted on his reputation and memory.

I desperately wanted to go to Jimi's funeral. But my parents, seeing the condition I was in, said they couldn't allow it. I pleaded with them to let Klaus-Peter come with me to take care of me, in case I collapsed at the funeral, but they refused to let me go.

I sank into a deep depression. The only escape I had left was to paint the "cross painting" Jimi had asked me to do. Because my father disapproved of me painting, I waited until my family went to bed and worked in the utility room or the cellar at night. While painting I felt close to Jimi – as if he was with me and supporting me.

Meanwhile my father was receiving anonymous letters, some of them saying the writers were glad this had happened to his daughter and Jimi Hendrix.

I found it hard to understand the irresponsible attitude of the newspapers, letting Jimi's fans believe he died of a drug overdose, and was a sex maniac and drug addict. These papers must have been aware of their influence. Throughout the years I have come across young people who admire Jimi's music. However, believing he was a hardened drug user, they tried to copy this, experimenting with drugs and in many cases getting hooked. The amount of tragedy caused by this continuous misinformation must be immeasurable.

The only person who offered to help me was Ed Chalpin, Jimi's former manager. At one point he asked me to fly to London, as he was sure he could set up some interviews for me. I flew to London but nothing materialized. Then, at the end of February, he told me to come to New York because he was convinced he could arrange interviews in some newspapers and magazines and maybe even on TV, but again nothing came of it.

While I was in New York I spoke to various people Jimi knew and found out that they believed Jimi had been murdered by Mike Jeffery. In their opinion Jimi was worth more to Jeffery dead than alive. As I said earlier, the day before his death Jimi had instructed his lawyer to terminate his management contract with Jeffery. Jeffery and Warner Brothers, the record company, each held a one-million-dollar life insurance policy on Jimi. Some of Jimi's friends believed he had come too close to finding out where all his money had disappeared. They said it was in Jeffery's interest to silence Jimi, who had made up his mind to leave him and who would have spoken out against him publicly.

These people, some of whom had been close to Jimi, were genuinely frightened of Jeffery. They told me that he had bought the silence of people with money or threats, while others had gone into hiding. I was also told that coming to New York had put my life in danger and that I should leave quickly, staying in my hotel room until it was time to go.

I realized that they were in earnest and that I should take these warnings seriously. They reminded me that Jeffery had Mafia connections, and I remembered all the things that Jimi had told me about him.

A few days later, on impulse, I left my room, drove to Greenwich Village and walked into the Electric Lady Studio. I saw people working on the building, changing some of the decorations. Everyone seemed to be staring at me. I finally entered Jeffery's room. At first he looked stunned to see me, but then he asked why I was in New York, and wanted to see the photographs of Jimi's last

days and my paintings. I told him I would get them. I knew what I was doing was unwise and dangerous, but I needed to know myself how far Jeffery would go.

After he had seen the photographs, he said we should make posters of them. He wanted me to sign a contract with him and told me I would make a lot of money out of this. (I had to hold myself back from telling him that I felt this was like making a contract with the devil himself.) I made an excuse, saying that I had no time to discuss it then as I was already late for another appointment.

All that day I wondered what to do. For safety's sake, I changed hotel.

The next day I phoned Jeffery and asked if he would come to my hotel room, where we could discuss things privately. He hesitated but then agreed. Once in my room he again talked about the contract he wanted me to sign. I accused him of buying people off and not revealing the truth about the real Jimi and how he really died.

Jeffery asked me how much I wanted. I told him I wanted the truth. He didn't take it seriously, thinking I was just trying to push up the price. He offered to pay me a large sum every month and to make me famous through my paintings – with him as my manager! He told me I should forget about the past and think about the future, again pressuring me to enter into a contract with him.

I felt very uncomfortable being in the same room as him, and remembering what harm he had done to Jimi. To someone who didn't know his true character, Jeffery might have seemed a kindly, soft-spoken person. However, Jimi and others had told me that this was one of his many tactics for manipulating people. He had an extremely cunning and inventive mind. As Chas Chandler said to the music journalist Chris Welch: "You didn't know

Sticks and stones Can't
break my soul
But words; They seem to
Sometimes harm me —

⊕ Maybe it's because
I'm forever hungry —

.... for the throth
of love

Precious Moment

how much you had been manipulated until you were out of his circle."

I told Jeffery I had to think about it, and that I would see him tomorrow. After he had left I was deeply relieved and knew I should leave New York at once. If I didn't sign the contract with him there was a strong possibility that he would use other methods to get his way.

The next day I called Jeffery and told him I had to fly to Seattle. He told me to contact him as soon as I came back, and I agreed, so as not to make him suspicious. That day a couple of other people who knew Jeffery and had seen what had been going on while Jimi was in New York, told me that they believed Jimi had been murdered. There were a couple of reasons for such a suspicion – one being that he had intended leaving Jeffery, the other that he was on the track of his manager's misappropriation of his money. I myself feel that there is a slight possibility Jimi was murdered, especially when I remember the unidentified compound found in his body, and Jeffery's past and the people he associated with.

At the same time I was told that there were certain groups and organizations like the FBI who must have considered Jimi a threat to society because of his potential for strong influence over the younger generation. They feared protest and rebellion, this fear probably strengthened by the fact that in a short time before Jimi's death something like a cult following had begun to build up around him in America.

I was told that some people were being persuaded and bribed to keep quiet and not tell the truth, in order to preserve Jimi's old image. In fact, Jimi was to be presented as someone with no interests apart from music, sex and drugs, as being unqualified to talk about any other matters. The

PEOPLE'S POWER

aim was to destroy Jimi's credibility by establishing and promoting a certain image around him. It was intended that people should think of him as the simple black man with no culture or refinement – a savage, an animal, rather than a human being, let alone a spiritual messenger.

Over the years there were quite a few individuals who, in their interests, exaggerated this negative picture of Jimi. Certain groups of people had their reasons to play down or even destroy Jimi's role as an important messenger. During his last eighteen months Jimi had been giving a number of rather weighty interviews to influential magazines and newspapers. In them he had given clear accounts of his beliefs about life, mankind, music and various other subjects. Anyone who takes the time to read these interviews carefully will find a highly intelligent person, speaking very critically about society and many essential aspects of human life. Jimi clearly unmasked the superficiality and careless brutality of the "plastic life" esteemed so highly by many, and which he intended to change.

When I arrived in Seattle, Jimi's father Al Hendrix, his wife Ayako June and their daughter Janie welcomed me in a very loving and kind way. We talked a lot about the time Jimi and I shared together and about the circumstances of Jimi's death.

We went to Jimi's grave, where I left a bunch of red roses. I have kept up my friendship with the Hendrix family over the years and continue to visit them. To this day Ayako June goes to Jimi's grave every month, being so kind as to leave a single red rose for him from me.

In March 1971 I went back to Germany, where I occupied myself with my paintings. In the meantime I had realized that if I wanted the truth to come out I would apparently have to write a book. One day I received a call from an associate of Jeffery's, who warned me to remain silent, or something might happen to me.

After an exhibition of my paintings in Düsseldorf, I left for London in July to stay in our rented flat in Notting Hill. For the next few months I worked on a manuscript for a book.

In both September and October someone broke into my flat. None of the windows was broken: it was as if someone had used a second key. Although no jewellery or money was stolen, the place had been searched in a really professional way. Nothing was in disarray, but the position of some items had been slightly altered. Fortunately, at that time most of the papers I had in connection with Jimi were in a bank safe, but not all of them, and some were missing. Luckily I had made copies of them and I used to carry my unfinished manuscript with me wherever I went. Obviously Jeffery was curious about what I was writing.

Soon afterwards I received a call from Jeffery himself. He told me that he had heard I was writing a book and that it would be healthier for me to forget about the idea, or something nasty could happen to me. I told him no one could stop me and hung up. A month later the manager (who does not want to be named) of a famous English rock band warned me that he had heard through

It was intended that people should think of him as the simple black man with no culture or refinement – a savage, an animal, rather than a human being, let alone a spiritual messenger.

When I arrived in Seattle, Jimi's father Al Hendrix, his wife Ayako June and their daughter Janie welcomed me in a very loving and kind way.

the grapevine that my life was in danger, He recommended that I should get some bodyguards and gave me a number to call.

I realized that things were getting serious. Now I understood even better why Jimi was so protective and worried about me all the time. A couple of months later Devon Wilson died in New York, allegedly from a drug overdose. Some people said it looked like a violent death and believed she was murdered.

Looking for a way out, I finally had an idea. I rang Jeffery and told him I had deposited my manuscript with a lawyer whom I had instructed to publish it in the event of my death. After that I never heard from him again.

A few months later I had a meeting with an

English businessman, who stole my manuscript. Only later did I find out that he had close connections with Jimi's manager.

In March 1973 Jeffery allegedly died in a plane crash on a flight to London, where he was to be questioned about the missing millions. To this day some people wonder whether he really died or used his intelligence expertise to make it look as if he had been on that plane, while disappearing to another country. Others believe it is possible that some of his associates had something to do with the crash in order to silence him.

I have never published a book until now. There are several reasons for this, but first of all I have to admit that I did not feel ready to expose myself to the public, by speaking about our love and the pain

Jimi's death has caused me. Each time I had to give an interview and talk about Jimi's death in detail, it felt as if someone was turning a knife in my heart.

I still did some interviews, as I felt very strongly that someone had to speak out for Jimi in a positive way and that people should learn the truth. Later I would find that parts of my interviews were omitted, or new parts added, distorting the whole story. Some newspapers and books even declared that I had given them an interview which had never taken place and they just printed what suited them. One book author pretended to have had an interview with me, and even acknowledged me in his book, although I had never spoken to him.

Watching this behaviour over the years eventually made me silent for a while. But I realized that this did not stop certain people from writing anything they wanted. So again I started giving interviews to various authors, hoping for some who wanted to find out about the real Jimi. However, many of them were mainly interested in writing what they thought fitted their preconceived idea of Jimi – someone they had never met in their life!

In this book I have described only a few of the main circumstances before and after Jimi's death. There is so much more to say, but it is beyond the book's scope to cover everything that happened at the time. However, there is one last incident that I feel I must mention. On 8 September 1991 a huge headline appeared on the front page of the *News of the World*, one of Britain's biggest-selling Sunday tabloids:

"HENDRIX CASE REOPENED"

The accompanying article stated that Scotland Yard was reopening the case of Jimi's death the next day because two "Miss Marple type fans" claimed to have proof that there had been a delay on my part in calling the ambulance on the morning Jimi died. One of these women said she talked to the two ambulance men who were in charge that day. They allegedly told her that the flat was empty. However, I was later told by one of the women that, when she had first asked one of the ambulance men if I had been at the flat, he said he remembered a girl being there. Yet at a later date he said he could not remember; and to both Scotland Yard and independent retired police superintendent Dennis Care he also said it was too long ago to remember whether someone was there

or not, but someone had let him into the flat. One of the women was a former girlfriend of Jimi's. The other one gave up after a while, realizing that nothing worthwhile and new, which had not already been said at the inquest in 1970, could be discovered about Jimi's death.

It was all a complete fabrication. Nothing was accurate: the headline was incorrect, the main thrust of the article was false, and the so-called investigation's outcome later turned out to be fiction. To say that the case was going to be reopened the next day was a blatant lie. A lie which sold newspapers but was never proved to be right – the case was never reopened.

Nevertheless, other newspapers and the television companies also started to spread this "news" all over the world. They soon found out that nothing about it was based on fact, so things soon died down again. But once more the true circumstances did not seem spectacular enough to be published, so many fans and other people were left believing that the case had been reopened and, to put it bluntly, that I had contributed to Jimi's death.

I felt very hurt at being accused of not having done all in my power to help Jimi when he most needed it. I would have given my life to save him. However, throughout the next two years the remaining amateur detective kept spreading these false accounts of events. Now she also alleged that not only the ambulance men, but also a policeman and a man called Mike Pergolani, supposedly a waiter at the Samarkand Hotel, had all stated that Jimi was already dead in the flat when the ambulance arrived. It was later discovered that there was no such person as Mike Pergolani working at the hotel.

The main statement in the woman's "report",

FIRST RAYS OF THE NEW RISING SUN

which had been sent to the UK's Attorney General, Sir Nicholas Lyell, was that Jimi died five hours earlier than had been stated by the coroner in 1970. I was stunned to discover that people seemed to believe these fantasies. This remaining "Miss Marple" even give a detailed interview to a *Jimi Hendrix Magazine* ("Why take five hours to call an ambulance?") repeating her false allegations, but making sure the identity of the ambulance men was withheld. She now constructed a most gruesome story of the circumstances of Jimi's death, allegedly based on the two ambulance men's statements. It was all invention, but it must have had a terrible effect on any Jimi Hendrix fan reading it.

Some time later, the same magazine called on all Jimi Hendrix fans to write to the Attorney General to press for the case to be reopened.

Writers of two books on Jimi which came out at the time – Tony Brown in *Jimi Hendrix* and Harry Shapiro, co-author of the Hendrix biography *Electric Gypsy* – repeated the false statements. They never bothered to check whether the ambulance men and the other "witnesses" had really made such statements or whether they were false or partly false. Instead it was all printed in these books, which were sold worldwide. Each edition of *Electric Gypsy* keeps changing the story of Jimi's death.

Finally, after two years, on 12 December 1993, Scotland Yard's International and Organised Crime Branch, headed by Detective Superintendent Douglas Campbell, was asked by the Attorney General to reinvestigate Jimi's death.

Again the news was spreading all over the world, but this time I felt pleased about it, being relieved that at last competent and experienced officers from Scotland Yard were looking into Jimi's death. I knew that they would come up with the truth, proving all the allegations and suspicions

to be false and unfounded.

Throughout these two years, which were a difficult period for me, Jimi's father Al Hendrix, Al's wife Ayako June and Jimi's sister Janie, as well as other relatives of Jimi, like Dolores Hall, stood by me, not having the slightest doubt about my credibility. I am still grateful for their unconditional faith.

Janie Hendrix visited me with her husband Troy and their youngest son while the investigation was going on, and also gave a TV interview in my support. And my own family, especially my mother and brother, and my friends, also helped me a lot during this painful time.

At the end of February 1994, Scotland Yard concluded their investigation and told me their findings. First, the ambulance men denied ever having said what had been attributed to them. They stated clearly that Jimi was alive when they arrived at the flat and also when they arrived at the hospital.

The policeman, Ian Smith, stated that he was at the flat, but never saw Jimi dead.

In the amateur detective's report the doctor who attended Jimi when he arrived at the casualty department, a Dr Bannister, maintained that he passed away earlier than had been stated at the inquest. He said the ambulance men had brought in "an unconscious patient who was dead on arrival" and that he suspected that Jimi had died many hours before. However, if Jimi had really been dead for such a long time, rigor mortis would have set in, and I have been told by doctors and the police that

any experienced nurse or doctor would have recognized this at once and would not have worked on such a person for 25-30 minutes, as stated by Dr Bannister himself. Wally Price, the admissions officer, also remembers that Jimi was treated by the doctor for about half an hour.

When I learned about this, I asked Scotland Yard what kind of doctor would work on a patient for such a long time while believing he had been dead for many hours. It makes me uncomfortable to think that this doctor had Jimi's life in his hands. Scotland Yard were unable to give me an answer, and simply informed me that they had found out that Dr Bannister had been struck off the medical register. Why he was struck off I have not been able to discover.

Dr Seifert, another doctor at St Mary Abbots, at first stated that he was called some time after Jimi's arrival at the hospital and that at the time he believed Jimi to be dead. However, in a statement which he had given previously in 1982, he had declared that he had forgotten the details of Jimi's death. In another statement he thought he was called to see Jimi perhaps five or ten minutes after his admission.

I remember well that on both occasions when I stepped into the treatment room Jimi was being worked on by one and the same doctor: Dr Bannister. Dr Bannister also stated that he vaguely remembered a blonde woman entering the treatment room. Moreover, Alvinia Bridges and I both clearly remember a nurse coming up to us, telling us that Jimi was alive.

> I felt very hurt at being accused of not having done all in my power to help Jimi when he most needed it.

They stated clearly that Jimi was alive when they arrived at the flat and also when they arrived at the hospital.

According to the woman's report, a pathologist hired by her had discovered, after checking the documents concerning the contents of Jimi's stomach, that he might have died five hours earlier than stated on the death certificate. However, when Scotland Yard had completed the reinvestigation, they explained to me that this pathologist's findings were inaccurate, as he had used an antiquated method and didn't have all the details. Scotland Yard's own pathologist also rechecked the findings of the pathologist who had carried out the original examination in 1970, and came to the conclusion that Jimi died at the same time as was first stated. Another eminent pathologist in England concluded likewise.

Only Dr Bannister kept giving confusing and contradictory statements. In his latest declaration he said: "I am unable to be precise whether he died in the Ambulance or at home." Another strange statement of his was that Jimi "had literally drowned himself in red wine". This was hardly possible, as the pathologist in 1970 had stated clearly that only about 100mg of alcohol, which is very little, had been in Jimi's blood at the time he took the sleeping tablets.

Naturally I too was asked to talk about the events of September 1970. It was towards the end of their investigation that Scotland Yard visited me, already making it clear that they were not deeming the "new" findings valid, but that the investigation had to be completed. My account, they later informed me, corroborated other testimony.

Many more witnesses were questioned during the reinvestigation, but those mentioned here were the key witnesses.

Scotland Yard submitted their findings to the Attorney General, and I myself asked them to include in their report the suggestion that the case should be reopened. I wanted everyone to hear once and for all, and publicly, the truth about the circumstances of Jimi's death, so that new rumours and speculation would not emerge again in a different form in the future.

Scotland Yard explained that they doubted that the Attorney General would reopen the case after reading their findings. It would mean a waste of taxpayers' money, as all the evidence they had gathered had pointed to the same conclusion as the inquest in 1970.

On 9 March 1994 the Attorney General made his decision public. His spokesman said: "The Attorney General has concluded in the light of all the evidence that there is not an appropriate case for the granting of consent."

A few months before Scotland Yard's fresh investigation, ex-Superintendent Dennis Care had carried out his own investigations with the authorization of Al Hendrix, who wanted an end to be put to all the rumours surrounding his son's death. Dennis Care talked to all the key witnesses and reached the same conclusions as Scotland Yard were soon to reach in their own reinvestigation.

However, history repeated itself. The allegations against me over those three months, provoked by the false information of the amateur detective, had been reported extensively all over the world. Now, the outcome of the reinvestigation, carried out and announced by Britain's most efficient and credible authorities, was not considered worthy of publication, except for a few lines in some of the newspapers.

The tune has changed, but the song remains the same. It had all already happened twenty-five years earlier, when an inquest vindicated Jimi both of having taken any hard drugs and of having died of a drug overdose. Yet nobody seemed to care.

What does all this prove? Clearly that the truth is not worth printing – only what seems shady and sensational. The facts of the matter are not to be

It makes me uncomfortable to think that this doctor had Jimi's life in his hands.

revealed, but instead are distorted beyond recognition. Jimi was not a drug victim. But his memory has become a victim of a coalition of ignorance and arrogance, of rumour and suspicion, of avarice and deceit.

Let us clear his name and honour his memory by seeing through the veil and acknowledging the real Jimi, and by understanding the essence of his life and his work. Nothing could be easier: just lean back, relax, listen to his music, read his lyrics and perhaps what he had to say in some of his interviews. Then a true picture will emerge in your mind and your heart. The picture of a loving soul, deeply moved by the world's fate, trying to contribute an important message to the welfare of mankind:

The message of Love.

THE COLOUR OF MUSIC

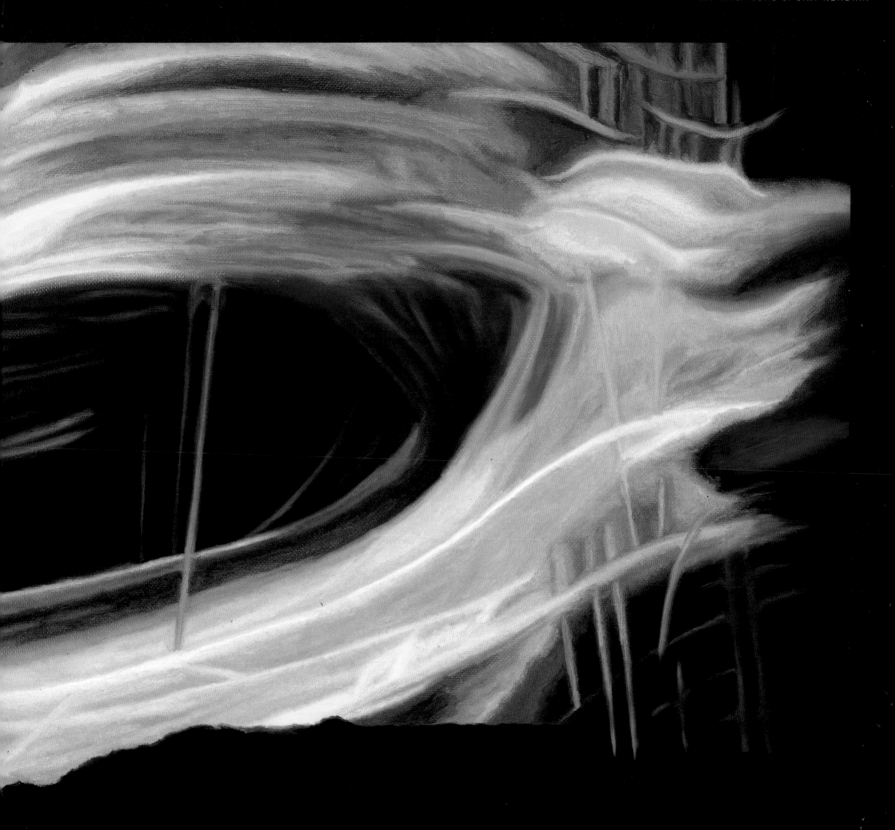

ACKNOWLEDGEMENTS

The author would like to thank James "Al" Hendrix for permission to reproduce examples of Jimi's handwriting and to use the photographs on pp10 and 185. Also, Ayako June Hendrix for permission to use the photograph on p13.

I gratefully acknowledge the permission of the following to reproduce copyright material: Copyright Bella Godiva Music Inc. (ASCAP) Administered for the World by Don Williams Music Group, Inc. All rights reserved. Used by permission. Jeff Levene; Tony Lopez; Claire Moriece; *Circus*; Nona Hatay; *Melody Maker*; *New Musical Express*; *Rolling Stone*; *Sounds*; *The Dick Cavett Show*; *The Tonight Show*/Flip Wilson; Time Inc.

I would also like to thank the following magazines and individuals with whom I was unable to make contact: *Beat Instrumental*; Nancy Carter; Sue Clark; *Disc and Music Echo*; Meatball Fulton; John Grant; *Hit Parade*; Jane de Mendelssohn (*International Times*); Mitch Mitchell; *Musical Express*; *Music Maker*; *Record Mirror*; *San Diego Free Press*; Alan Smith; *TeenSet*; Sheila Weller.

The following poems are Copyright © Monika Dannemann 1995: "For you my love I dedicate" (p28); "I come running home to you Jupiter" (p104); "Mighty Eagles" (p147); "The Story of Life" (p171).

I would like to give special thanks to the following photographers for permission to use their photographs for reference for my paintings: Steve Azzara (p45); Douglas Kent Hall (pp89, 124); Nona Hatay, author of Jimi Hendrix Reflections and Visions, a Pomegranate Artbook (pp7, 174); Mark Haywood (p90); Cornelius Hudulla (p134); Allan Koss (pp54, 71, 80, 119, 128, 132, 190); Bill Nitopi's Collection (pp38, 43, 65, 77, 99, 109, 127).

I acknowledge the permission of the following to partially base paintings on their photographs: Ed Caraeff (p33); Laurens van Houten (pp31, 37, 75, 95); Jean-Pierre Leloir (p68); London Features International Ltd (pp61, 107); David Redfern (pp2, 85, 103, 114); Joe Sia (pp83, 97, 111, 182, 183, 186).

I also want to thank those photographers whom I was unable to contact.

The photographs on the following pages are Copyright © Monika Dannemann 1995: pp15, 25, 51, 53, 73, 105, 137, 139, 143.